D1049961

A COMPLETE INTRODUCTION TO
ZEBRA FINCHES

Normal Grey Zebra Finches.

A COMPLETE INTRODUCTION TO
ZEBRA FINCHES

COMPLETELY ILLUSTRATED IN FULL COLOR

Zebra Finches originated in Australia and are now widely bred by waxbill enthusiasts.

John L. Corbett

Photographs: L. Arnall, 62. Dr. Herbert R. Axelrod, 20. Chelman & Petrulla, 25. Kerry V. Donnelly, 36. Terry Dunham, 52. Michael Gilroy, 18. Ray Hanson, 28, 55, 65. Dr. M. Heidenreich, 70–71. I.F. Keymer, 68. Paul Kwast, 64. Harry V. Lacey, 2–3, 5, 8–9, 17, 47, 77, 81, 94–95. Dan Martin, 69. Louise Van der Meid, 37, 39, 42. N. Richmond, 35. Mervin F. Roberts, 1, 29–30, 34, 43–45, 51, 54, 56–57, 59. Heinz Schrempp, 72. W.A. Starika, 16, 58. Courtesy of Vogelpark Walsrode, 22–23, 48–49, 53, 63, 66–67, 73–80, 82–89. J. Wessels, 19, 46.

Distributed in the UNITED STATES by T.F.H. Publications, Inc., 211 West Sylvania Avenue, Neptune City, NJ 07753; in CANADA to the Pet Trade by H & L Pet Supplies Inc., 27 Kingston Crescent, Kitchener, Ontario N2B 2T6; Rolf C. Hagen Ltd., 3225 Sartelon Street, Montreal 382 Quebec; in CANADA to the Book Trade by Macmillan of Canada (A Division of Canada Publishing Corporation), 164 Commander Boulevard, Agincourt, Ontario M1S 3C7; in ENGLAND by T.F.H. Publications Limited, 4 Kier Park, Ascot, Berkshire SL5 7DS; in AUSTRALIA AND THE SOUTH PACIFIC by T.F.H. (Australia) Pty. Ltd., Box 149, Brookvale 2100 N.S.W., Australia; in NEW ZEALAND by Ross Haines & Son, Ltd., 18 Monmouth Street, Grey Lynn, Auckland 2 New Zealand; in SINGAPORE AND MALAYSIA by MPH Distributors (S) Pte., Ltd., 601 Sims Drive, #03/07/21, Singapore 1438; in the PHILIPPINES by Bio-Research, 5 Lippay Street, San Lorenzo Village, Makati Rizal; in SOUTH AFRICA by Multipet Pty. Ltd., 30 Turners Avenue, Durban 4001. Published by T.F.H. Publications Inc. Manufactured in the United States of America by T.F.H. Publications, Inc.

Contents

Introduction

The Zebra Finch, *Taeniopygia guttata,* is probably the most widely kept cage or aviary bird, after the budgerigar and the canary. Such popularity is not difficult to understand for such a charming little bird, which has many attributes. It is relatively hardy and may be kept in outside aviaries all year 'round in most climates, providing a frostfree and draft-proof shelter is available.

It has extremely attractive plumage, which comes in several color varieties, and it breeds readily and easily in captivity. All this, coupled with its comical and endearing "tin trumpet" call, makes it one of our best loved avian home companions.

The founding of societies specializing in Zebra Finches—in the United Kingdom, the United States and Australia—has further increased the popularity of these birds, which have proven

A pair of Normal Grey Zebra Finches. The male is more colorful possessing an orange patch on each cheek, and a white spotted chestnut patch on each flank.

An example of the color possibilities of the Zebra Finch. Males of the Fawn and Grey varieties are still discernible by their more colorful cheek patches. The White males possess a deeper hued bill.

excellent subjects for exhibition; much competition exists between breeders to produce show-bench winners.

Another feature, of considerable importance to many potential aviculturists, is that the birds are relatively inexpensive to purchase. Even excellent exhibition stock is often well within the finances of the average enthusiast, especially when compared with other species. Also, Zebra Finches are economical to keep; they do not require expensive foodstuffs, and adequate housing for your stock should not prove financially prohibitive. It is the purpose of this book to introduce the beginner to Zebra Finches, and to cover all aspects of keeping and breeding these delightful little birds.

History and Classification

The Normal, or Grey male Zebra Finch; throat and upper breast are zebra striped.

The wild Zebra Finch is found in most parts of continental Australia, being absent from Arnhem Land, the Cape York Peninsula in northern Queensland and certain areas along the eastern and southern coasts. It does not occur in Tasmania, but is found in a number of East Indian islands, notably Sumba and Timor in the Flores group. Not surprisingly, with such a great range of distribution, a number of geographical races, or subspecies, occur showing slight differences in color and markings. Thirteen subspecies are recognized at present, but undoubtedly further races will be discovered and described in the future.

Small groups of a dozen or more Zebras may be seen in suitable habitats, although they may sometimes congregate in groups of many hundreds. They prefer grass and scrubland, never too far from a water source, but may increase their range after heavy rainfall. They are extremely active and wary, busily working their way through the grasses and shrubs, feeding mainly on seeds and other vegetation. In some areas, they are classed as agricultural pests and measures are taken to control them. There is no precise breeding season, but they seem to be encouraged to nest by the onset of rain.The nest is an untidy affair, composed of grass, foliage and feathers. It may be constructed in a hole in a tree, a rock crevice, or in dense foliage, and much squabbling will occur in the selection of the most favorable sites.

Evolution of the Zebra Finch

Before discussing Zebra Finches in particular, it is worth considering the general evolution of all birds, which will hopefully lead the reader to a better understanding of his/her chosen subject. What does the word *evolution* mean? In the dictionary at hand, it is described as "the act of unrolling or unfolding; gradual working out or development; the doctrine according to which higher forms of life have gradually arisen out of the lower." There are other meanings to the word, but the one which we require is the last one mentioned here. "Gradually arisen" is the operative phrase, which can be described almost as an understatement; evolution from one form to another may take millions of years!

Charles Darwin (1809–1882) was among the first to expound a theory of evolution by natural selection, and a great deal of controversy arose, particularly from the religious communities, when his famous book, *On The Origin of Species,* was published in 1859. In the book, Darwin attempted to prove that the higher and more complex forms of life gradually arose by a succession of small changes,

A pair of Chestnut-flanked White Zebra Finches. The female is depicted at top.

from the lower and simpler forms. Of particular interest to the Zebra Finch enthusiast is the fact that a portion of Darwin's studies included the different island races of Galapagos finches.

It is generally considered that the birds (and also the mammals, for that matter) arose from certain primitive reptiles. Let us consider a simple theory as to how this could have come about. Certain small lizard-like reptiles which were vulnerable to larger carnivorous predators will have climbed into trees in order to escape from them. Eventually, the predators developed sufficiently to be able to chase their prey into the trees. The prey developed one step further by leaping from one tree to another or to the ground; those which were not quick enough became victims.

Dark Fawn pair; various shades and highlights can be produced in this color group.

cover considerable distances through the air.

The power of flight had already been developed by the invertebrates (insects), but the requirements of flight in the vertebrates were more complex. The flying animal had to be able to overcome the pull of gravity. It had to be comparatively light in weight, which it accomplished by developing hollow bones, and the wing size had to be sufficient to support the whole body. It had to have powerful forelimb muscles to

It follows that those with the most convenient weight and shape were able to leap further and faster than the others, which gradually became extinct. From generation to generation, piece by piece, those little mutations which were favorable to the survival of the species gradually developed: digits lengthened and became webbed, flaps of skin along the body appeared, and the leapers became parachutists and gliders, being able to

operate the wings, which meant that the breast bone had to be enlarged for attachment of these muscles.

The first vertebrate animals with the complete power of flight were the flying reptiles known as pterosaurs which appeared in the early Jurassic period, about 190 million years ago. These had a superficially bird-like skeleton; a large number of fossil species have been described, some of which had a wingspan of 15 meters (50

The male Silver Zebra Finch has a light cream cheek patch.

feet) or more! The pterosaurs became extinct toward the end of the Cretaceous period, about 70 million years ago. It is thought that these great flying reptiles were unable to withstand the competition from the birds, which began to evolve in the late Jurassic period (about 140 million years ago), and had reached a high state of development by the end of the Cretaceous. Like the pterosaurs, the birds evolved from reptiles, but there is no fossil evidence to prove a connection between the two, other than a common ancestry. The birds evolved in a different way, the body scales developing into feathers, which not only assisted in the power of flight, but insulated the body and retained heat, thus increasing the metabolic rate, thereby making more energy available and increasing efficiency.

Fossil remains of birds are scarce, and the earliest known types were discovered in the Solnhofen limestone of Bavaria, Germany. Two complete skeletons and a number of part skeletons are remarkably preserved, and even show the feathers—the absence of which would have resulted in these fossils being classified as reptiles, as they still possesed a number of reptilian characteristics. This first bird was called *Archaeopteryx* and was about the size of a crow; it was an intermediate form between the reptiles and the birds, showing characteristics of each, yet it is generally considered as the first member of the class Aves.

History and Classification

During the Cretaceous period, birds made considerable evolutionary progress, and by the beginning of Cenozoic times (65 million years ago), they were almost completely modernized. They had reached their present stage of complex skeletal structure, and there seems to have been little structural change since. Differences in habitat, however, led the birds to become one of the most diverse classes of vertebrate animals, with over 8,500 living species inhabiting almost every corner of the earth— from the oceans to the mountain peaks, and from the polar regions to the equatorial rain forests. Adaptations to the different habitats have led birds to develop a remarkable diversity of form and color. As examples, take the huge, flightless ostrich of the African savannah and the tiny hummingbirds of the Americas.

By far the most successful order of birds is the Passeriformes, which contains four suborders and numerous families. Our subject, the Zebra Finch, has evolved as a member of this order. To help better understand how this species fits into the complex structure of evolution, it is worth taking a brief look at classification.

Classification of the Zebra Finch

Before logical classifications of plants and animals were attempted, natural historians had a great deal of trouble separating the species, particularly those which were closely related and similar in form and color. It was the Swedish biologist Karl von Linné, generally known as Linnaeus (1707–1778), who devised the first "logical" system of classification.

A Fawn Penguin cock, the result of interbreeding both Fawn and Penguin Zebra Finches.

Known as the *binomial system* of nomenclature, every plant and animal species known was designated with a double name, the first being the *generic* name, the second being the *specific* name. As Latin was the language mainly used internationally by scholars at that time, it was the language most often used for the binomials, though a fair proportion of Greek and other languages may appear in zoological nomenclature. Taking a simple example, the horse was named *Equus caballus,* the first name being the genus to which the horse belongs, the second name designating the horse specifically. Other species in the horse genus, such as the zebra (which, it is thought, is appropriate to use as an example here), have the same generic name but a different specific name, e.g. *Equus burchelli.*

Species and genera are placed into larger categories, based on similarities and differences, in ascending order. Thus, a species is contained within a genus, a genus within a family, a family within a class and so on. In some difficult cases of classification, categories such as subfamilies or infraorders may be used, but these are usually optional, dependent on the judgment of the particular author. The science of the classification of living organisms is known as *taxonomy,* and those who study this discipline are called *taxonomists.* Due to the complexity of life, it is inevitable that difficulty may be experienced in classifying certain creatures which are similar to each other. Controversy frequently occurs amongst taxonomists as to how a particular species should be classified. The

The female Normal Penguin is darker than the Fawn Penguin variety.

Zebra Finch, which we will now turn to as the subject of this book, has not escaped this controversy, and it has had at least six scientific names in its short history.

The first scientific description of the Zebra Finch was made by the French

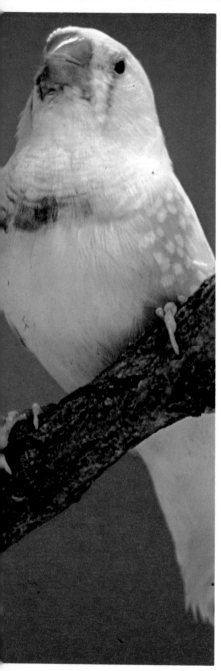

Cheek patches on the male Chestnut-flanked White are subtler but still apparent.

zoologist Viellot in 1817, when he named it *Fringilla guttata.* In 1837, the naturalist and explorer Gould called it *Amadina castanotis,* in his *Synopsis of the Birds of Australia.* Subsequently he renamed it *Taeniopygia castanotis,* but this was again changed to *Poephila guttata* by those who disagreed with him. Since then, it has been called *Poephila castanotis,* and has even been relegated to subspecific rank as *Taeniopygia guttata castanotis* or *Poephila guttata castanotis.* Most modern ornithologists use either *Poephila guttata* or *Taeniopygia guttata;* the former term would relegate it to a genus containing other Australian grass-finches, while the latter puts the Zebra Finch in a genus of its own. As the Zebra Finch shows certain unique characteristics not shared by other members of the genus *Poephila,* the name *Taeniopygia guttata* will be the one employed for this book.

As a matter of interest, the meanings of the scientific names given above are as follows: *castanotis* = "chestnut-colored ear" (relating to certain areas of the bird); *Fringilla* = "finch"; *guttata* = "spotted"; *Poephila* = "grass loving" and *Taeniopygia* = "banded rumped." Binomials are always written with the initial letter of the generic name capitalized, with the second, specific, name always being

A pair of Normal Grey Zebra Finches.

The male Fawn Zebra Finch.

The Normal, Wild, or Grey Zebra Finch.

lower cased, even when derived from a proper name. Using the binomial *Taeniopygia guttata,* the Zebra Finch is classified within the animal kingdom as follows:

KINGDOM: Animalia (all animals, as opposed to plants)

PHYLUM: Chordata (all animals with a dorsal nervous system)

CLASS: Aves (all birds; i.e. animals with feathers)

ORDER: Passeriformes (the "perching birds," the largest order containing over 5,000 species in 75 families)

FAMILY: Estrildidae (including Java Sparrows, mannikins, grass-finches, Zebra Finches, and waxbills).

SUBFAMILY: Erythrurini (Zebra Finches, grass-finches, parrot-finches, Gouldian Finches)

GENUS: *Taeniopygia* (Zebra Finches)

SPECIES: *Taeniopygia guttata* (Zebra Finch)

About thirteen subspecies of Zebra Finch are recognized. These consist of geographical races, which exhibit slight differences, yet enough to warrant subspecific rankings. When a subspecies is described, a subspecific name is added to the binomial, making a *trinomial,* e.g. *Taeniopygia guttata guttata* and *Taeniopygia guttata castanotis.*

Accommodation

Zebra Finches are among the easiest of all pet birds to accommodate. Unlike parrot-like birds, they will not gnaw at the woodwork and cause damage. Unlike many softbills, which have rather messy droppings, those of the healthy Zebra Finch are relatively dry and inoffensive. Due to their small size, Zebra Finches do not require voluminous housing; a pair will do well, even breed, in a cage 60cm (2ft) long × 30cm (1ft) deep × 35cm (1¼ft) high, although this should be the very minimum size for a pair.

Before acquiring any stock, it is advisable to decide whether you intend to keep your Zebras in cages or an aviary. The average fancier will probably start off with a single pair of birds, which he will keep in a small cage. Unlike budgerigars or

Special consideration should be spent on the choosing of an appropriate Zebra Finch cage. Bars must be closely spaced to avoid the escape or possible strangulation of birds.

canaries, Zebra Finches should not be kept singly. They are gregarious birds and, although they can become very tame and trusting towards their owners, they never seem to accept humans as a substitute for their own kind, as some of the aforementioned species do; so every Zebra Finch should always have at least one other Zebra Finch for company. Always arrange the housing for the birds before you acquire them. Various points may have to be discussed with the family; many an argument has developed over a member of the family arriving home with a couple of birds in a cardboard transport box, which he has bought on impulse. Never buy livestock on impulse! Not only can this lead to family arguments, it is often most detrimental to the livestock in question.

Cages

If you intend to start with just one pair of pet Zebras, these can be kept in a small cage in the living room. A good-sized

cage which gives the birds plenty of room for exercise would be 1m (3¼ft) long × 60 cm (2ft) high × 45cm (1½ft) deep, and there would be enough room to acquire another pair of birds later if you wish. The all-metal "bell-" or box-shaped cages, which are available in pet shops and are intended for budgerigars, parrots or canaries, are unsuitable for Zebra Finches, since it would be difficult to obtain one with gaps between the wires narrow enough to prevent the Zebras from squeezing through. Additionally, small birds never seem to accept being "open" to view on all sides, in the same way as do budgies and canaries, and thus are likely to panic every time somebody approaches the cage. Consequently, by far the best kind of cage for Zebra Finches is one which is enclosed by a solid "wall" on all sides, except the front. Such cages may be purchased readymade, but if you are a handy person, it is much more fun to construct your own. The floor, top and back can be constructed from plywood 7.5mm (¼ in) thick, the ends from 15mm (½ in) plywood. The former can be glued and tacked onto the latter to form a strong construction. Wire fronts of various sizes can be purchased from your local pet shop or from avicultural suppliers; it is then a simple matter to construct the cage according to the size of the front.

The cage fronts are usually fitted with a door and a couple of spaces for food and water containers. Alternatively, the door may be constructed in one of the ends. Door catches should be fashioned in such a way that they can be adequately secured and, if one has small children, it is best to fit some kind of lock, to prevent any sudden and unwelcome escapes by the birds. To facilitate cleaning, a sliding

Wooden perches or natural branches are preferable and should be cleaned routinely with a commercially available perch scraper.

floor tray is usually fitted in the base of the cage. This can consist of a sheet of thin plywood, or thin sheet metal, mounted on a frame constructed from batten of about 1cm x 1cm (½ in x ½ in) in section. Enough space should be left at the bottom of the wire front to allow the tray to be easily slid in and out. The advantage of such a tray is that the floor of the cage can be cleaned without undue disturbance to the birds.

Perches are best fashioned from natural twigs and

branches, which will give your Zebras the benefit of various thicknesses. Special dowel rods, available from pet shops, are useful to have at either end of the cage, so that the birds have a solid base on

A Pied Grey female; Pieds can be produced in all colors of the Zebra Finch.

which to rest when they are flying backwards and forwards, but such perches alone are considered not good for the birds' feet. The advantage of natural twigs as perches is that they may be changed as soon as they become soiled—and they should be scrubbed and washed before use, to remove any potentially dangerous wild bird droppings or other pollutants. Care should be

taken not to include the twigs of poisonous trees, yew and laburnum being the main ones to avoid. The twigs of fruit trees are probably best, and a few leaves or buds may be left on them to give the birds something to nibble at.

The floor of the cage is best covered with a sprinkling of clean sand. Rather than using sand which you have collected yourself, or builders sand, it is advisable to purchase special bird sand from your pet shop. This is specially cleaned and treated, and can be obtained with a grit and trace-element additive, which will be beneficial to your birds' health. The sand will absorb the fluid part of the droppings and is more hygienic than other floor coverings such as sheets of paper or sandpaper. The sand should be changed at regular intervals, depending on how quickly it becomes soiled, but every other day should be adequate when one has only a single pair of birds in the cage.

Aviaries
Being colony birds, Zebra Finches are ideal for keeping in groups in outdoor aviaries. These birds are reasonably docile and, although pairs can become a little pugnacious during breeding time, if enough space and nest boxes are available, it is quite safe to keep them in a community with other bird species of similar size and temperament. Although Zebras are

surprisingly hardy, and can be kept outside all year 'round in most climates, it is imperative that they have access to a draft-proof and frost-proof shelter. If the temperature does not reach as low as freezing point, one can make do with the absolute minimum of heating arrangements.

There is almost no limit to the number of types and sizes of aviaries suitable for Zebra Finches. Aviaries can be bought in sections ready to erect, with the minimum of fuss, or it is possible to construct your own aviary to your own design. Whatever you do, careful planning must be the first consideration. Choose the site in your garden which you think will be most suitable for an aviary. Normally it should be situated where it will receive maximum sunshine, but at the same time, it should be protected from harsh winds. The best way to do this is to have the aviary in front of the south-facing wall (in the northern hemisphere, of course) of a building. Alternatively a thick, windbreaker hedge or a high fence may be used.

Before erecting any structure, even if it is on your own land, ensure that you will not be violating any local regulations; in some areas of some countries it may be necessary to obtain building permission from the local authorities. Also, it is a good idea to obtain approval from your neighbors at the outset, rather than risk receiving

complaints about blocking the view or excessive noise at a later date. Admittedly, Zebra Finches are not renowned for keeping people awake, but there are some people who can be quite uncooperative

A young Pied Grey male will develop more striking plumage as it matures.

when it comes dealing with their neighbors' hobbies.

While an aviary may be erected on almost any piece of land, obviously the more level it is, the easier it will be to lay the foundations and to get the panels to fit. It is always worth going to the trouble of laying a solid foundation before erecting an aviary, for two good reasons. Firstly, it will prevent predators and vermin from

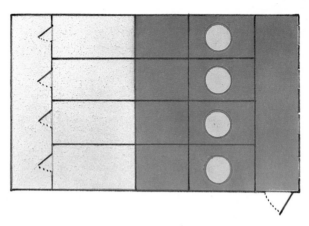

A four-section aviary, displaying a main entrance area doubling as a safety porch. The brown area depicts the indoor shelter; the blue, the screened outdoor flight area.

burrowing into the aviary and creating havoc among your stock; secondly, it will mean that the timber structure of the aviary will not come in direct contact with the soil, thus reducing the possibility of rotting. Once you have decided on the size of the aviary, you can dig your foundation trench; this will go all around the aviary perimeter, including the shelter. Let us imagine that we are going to construct an aviary with a flight 4m × 2m (13ft × 6½ft) and a shelter 2m × 2m (6½ft × 6½ft), which would easily accommodate ten or more pairs of Zebra Finches. The foundation trench is dug to a depth and width of 30cm (1ft) and, for the aviary in question, would be 6m (19½ft) along each side and 2m (6½ft) along each end, allowing for the aviary framework to run along the center. By using wooden pegs, a straight edge and a spirit level, find a constant level all the way around. Concrete—a mixture of one part cement, two parts sand and four parts gravel—should be laid in the trench to the level of the pegs and tamped down with a flat piece of timber. Allow twenty-four hours for the concrete to set before building a low wall, from bricks or blocks, to the exact size of the aviary.

The area taken up by the shelter should preferably be concreted all over. Be sure to lay a sheet of plastic or other damp-proofer on the ground before doing so. The height of the wall is a matter of taste, but about 30cm (1ft) is probably the average. Do not forget to leave a space in the shelter end for the access door; the door to the flight can be mounted on top of the wall. In order to secure the framework to the wall, a number of bolts, fixed into the cement between the bricks and pointing vertically upwards, are placed at intervals of about 30cm (1ft).

Panels for aviaries may be purchased from your avicultural suppliers. These are usually 1m × 2m or 3ft × 6ft, depending where you obtain them. After drilling holes in the bottom framework, to fit the bolts protruding from the wall, the panels are bolted into a vertical position. Each panel is drilled and bolted to the next one, and finally the roof panels are bolted on.

Purchased panels are usually already covered with galvanized wire mesh. For Zebra Finches you will require

a mesh size not greater than 12mm (½ inch); otherwise the birds may attempt to escape. In addition, a small mesh will prevent mice and other unwanted pests from entering the aviary.

The shelter part of the aviary may also be constructed with a timber framework, but instead of covering it with mesh, it is totally enclosed using tongue-and-groove boarding or shiplap. The inside of the shelter may be lined with plywood or hardboard which can be painted with a leadfree emulsion paint. By painting the inside of the shelter with a light-colored paint the light will be enhanced, and it will facilitate cleaning. The roof of the shelter should slope away from the outside flight and should be covered with

Warm-climate aviaries in a serene backyard retreat.

roofing felt or other waterproof material. If transparent plastic roof coverings are used, care should be taken to install adequate ventilation facilities within the shelter, as oven-like conditions can prevail in hot weather.

If you have enough room, it is best to leave a corridor inside the shelter, into which you can enter without entering the indoor flight, which is covered with mesh just like the outdoor flight. With such additional space there will be room to store extra cages,

Showing more detail is the male Marked White or Marmosette Zebra Finch.

feed and equipment, and you will have somewhere to work in inclement weather, without unduly disturbing the birds. Adequate windows should be installed in the shelter to admit as much natural light as possible. If the windows are installed in areas to be occupied by birds, they must be protected with mesh frames on the inside, to prevent the birds from flying into the glass and injuring themselves. In addition to this, it may be possible to rig up a means of opening the windows in hot weather for ventilation, without letting the birds escape.

The pophole, through which the birds will pass from the shelter to the outside flight and vice versa, should be situated fairly high up in the wall of the shelter. The hole need not be greater than 15cm x 15cm (6in x 6in), and a shelf should be fitted at its base for the birds to land and take off as they use it. A sliding door should be fitted into grooves along the sides of the pophole; this can be operated by a chain from outside the aviary, somewhat in the manner of a portcullis. If the sliding door is made from a heavy piece of sheet metal, it is most unlikely to jam in the runner. Alternatively, the door can run horizontally across the opening. A rod is attached to it, and it is simple to open and close it from outside the aviary. When opening and closing such doors, care should be taken to ensure that no birds are trapped.

Some fanciers like to lock their birds into the shelter each night, and this is not a bad idea in the winter. However, it is not recommended during the breeding season, as the birds will be disturbed, and they usually want to start foraging around in the flight at dawn. If you have a number of attached aviaries and shelters, it may be useful to have additional popholes between the shelters, which will facilitate moving or catching up birds when necessary.

Heating and Lighting
Zebra Finches are extremely hardy and can be allowed to use outdoor flights all the year 'round in most climates. They will usually go voluntarily into the shelter at night, and all that is required is that this area remains free of temperatures below freezing. A small electric tubular heater will be adequate for the average small shelter and will ensure a frost-free environment.

Lighting is a different matter, for the short winter day in some areas allow the birds insufficient time to feed themselves adequately. Especially when the birds are breeding they should have not less than twelve hours of light per day in which they can perform their essential duties for raising their broods. In most shelters, a single

A Marked White or Marmosette female showing only the slightest markings on her white plumage: the teardrop under the eye.

fluorescent tube, preferably of the "daylight" type, can be left on in the evening in order to extend the period of light. Some breeders like to make this extended period of artificial daylight more natural by installing a system of dimmers and timers which will not only switch the lights on and off at the required times but also simulate dawn and dusk with the dimming effect.

Decorating the Aviary
An aviary can be made to look extremely attractive; with Zebra Finches, it is possible to have a display of plants and

shrubs inside the aviary as well as around it. For purposes of shelter from strong winds, a thick hedge may be planted around the parts of the aviary which are yew, parts of which could fall into the aviary and be ingested by the birds, with disastrous results.

Climbing plants, such as honeysuckle, clematis or

A variety of aviaries can be designed to house Zebra Finches. Consideration must be given to heating in an aviary built in colder climates.

not protected structurally. Any form of hardy evergreen will be useful for this purpose and can include privet, box, cotoneaster or one of the fast-growing conifers. To break up the straight outlines of the aviary, one or two additional trees or shrubs can be planted near the corners. Beware of the poisonous trees such as laburnum or

jasmine, may be trained to grow up the aviary posts, but these should pe pruned well each winter to prevent their doing damage to the aviary mesh.

The floor of the aviary is best covered with a layer of good-quality turf, which is clipped or mowed at regular intervals, but leaving a few clumps to go to seed. One or two shrubs may be planted inside the aviary, again ensuring that nothing poisonous is used. It is not wise to allow the interior of the flight to become too overgrown for several reasons. For one thing, you will not see too much of the birds if they are flitting about in thick foliage. Also, trees and shrubs allowed to grow

intervals.

A few rocks and rock plants in the aviary can look attractive, especially if a shallow pond is installed at their base, in which the birds

unchecked will soon grow through the mesh of the aviary wire and distort it, in some cases breaking it and allowing birds to escape. If the foliage is excessively thick, you may not even see this happening until it is too late. A third reason is that you will want your birds to nest in the boxes provided, and not build at random in the shrubs, which they certainly will do if given the chance. Therefore, although it is nice to have decorative plants inside the aviary, they must be tended and pruned at regular

All birds prefer perching on natural branches. Choose branches that are free from pesticide sprays. Scraping with a perch cleaner helps to keep them hygienic.

can bathe. It is quite easy to make a small, natural-looking pool, using a few rocks, a sheet of plastic and some concrete. The rocks are arranged to the rough shape of the pool, and the plastic is placed flat in the center, with the edges coming up the sides of the rocks. Having ensured that all the rocks are embedded firmly into the

This window-mounted aviary is covered on the sides with sheet plastic to provide protection from the elements.

ground, the gaps between them are filled with cement

mortar. A large dollop of concrete (which has not been mixed too wet) is placed in the center of the plastic sheet and worked outwards with a trowel, until a basin-like structure has been formed in the rocks and the plastic is totally covered with the concrete. By gently stroking the surface of the still-wet concrete with a soft

out frequently during the summer months, as it will quickly become fouled with fallen leaves and bird droppings as well as the dirt

Plants can provide aesthetic appeal, as well as providing natural perches and shade from the sun.

handbrush, a smooth surface can be made. Such a pond for Zebra Finches should never be more than 5cm (2in) deep, as there would be a danger of birds drowning, particularly recent fledglings. A pond should be emptied or covered over in the winter, as birds may deside to take a bath when the water is just above freezing and give themselves hypothermia when they return to the cold wind.

The pond must be cleaned

which the birds carry into it. A pond should be placed in an open part of the aviary and obviously not directly below a shrub or perch.

In addition to the trees and shrubs which may be planted in the aviary, a number of "permanent" perches should be fixed at strategic positions, both in the shelter and in the flight. The author has found bamboo canes, of the type supplied for gardeners to stake their plants, to be ideal as perches. They are long-lasting and come in various lengths and thicknesses. Perches should be fixed securely so that they do not rotate when the birds land on them. They should be placed at varying heights, but never one directly above the other. It is better to place two or three perches at each end of the flight, allowing a long flight path in between them to give your birds maximum exercise.

Aviary Maintenance

All timber used in aviary construction should receive a good coating of wood preservative, paying particular attention to those parts which will be inaccessible when the aviary is built, such as the insides of joints and the bottoms of frames. It is now possible to purchase special preservatives which are non-poisonous to animals or plants but will destroy the organisms which cause wood to rot. These compounds come in a variety of colors and, in the author's opinion,

Scrutinize the building plans before aviary construction gets underway. A safety porch should be added to this design to prevent accidental escapes.

are more attractive than paint, as they enhance rather than hide the grain of the timber and are also less stark in appearance. If the new aviary

Aviaries can be designed to fit available space. Different species of birds may be kept in each of these four compartments.

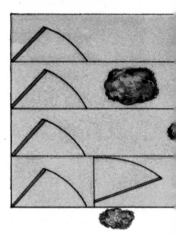

receives a good coat of preservative at the outset, it will not require a maintenance coat until two years later. When applying the maintenance coat to the aviary, it is advisable to remove the birds, so the best time to do this is in late fall, after the breeding season has ended. The birds can either be locked inside the shelter or placed in cages for the duration of the maintenance. The preservative should be thoroughly dry before the birds are released back into the flight.

In addition to daily feeding, Make certain that everything has thoroughly dried out before reintroducing the birds.

One problem which occurs in indoor flights and birdrooms is the continual build-up of dust, consisting of fine particles of birdseed,

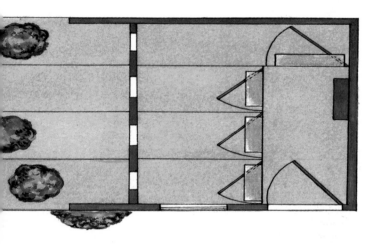

cleaning and inspection, a thorough cleaning of the inside shelter should be made once per week. All sand, droppings and other mess should be cleaned off the floor and the walls and perches scrubbed and wiped down with soapy water. At intervals of twelve months, the shelter should be more thoroughly cleaned out and washed down with a solution of bleach in warm water, which is then rinsed off with clean, warm water. The bleach will kill off any germs or parasites which are lurking in the cracks and crevices. When the walls have dried, a new coat of emulsion paint may be applied if necessary.

sand, droppings and feathers. If allowed to build up unchecked, this dust can have a detrimental effect on the birds, as they are continually inhaling it as it floats about in the air. A moderately recent innovation for use in the bird room is the negative air ionizer which effectively kills all viruses, bacteria and fungal spores in the air and causes dust to settle. Working by electricity, such an ionizer is inexpensive to buy, cheap to run and a definite advantage to the birds and their keeper due to the vastly improved environment. Enquire about the negative air ionizer at your avicultural supplier.

Feeding

The feeding of Zebra Finches should present no special problems; providing your birds receive a balanced diet and are kept in hygienic conditions, they will thrive. What then is a balanced diet? It may be a good idea to look at generalized nutrition here first, so that one can gain a better understanding of the bird's requirements.

To remain in the best of health all living things require a diet containing the basic dietary constituents of proteins, carbohydrates, fats, vitamins, mineral salts and the ever-important water. The infinite variety of mammals, birds, reptiles, amphibians, fishes and invertebrates all have to have these dietary constituents if they are to continue to be successful. And they all have to get them from somewhere. In fact, they get them from each other and, if you look around and think about it, there is not a single living organism that could survive without other living things. Many animals have become specialized in

Zebra Finches should be fed an assortment of seeds each day.

the way they seek their food; one only has to look at the vast number of different avian bills, each one of which has evolved to exploit a particular range of food items. The sturdy little bill of the Zebra Finch is fashioned to extract

Most commercially packaged canary products can be used for finches. Check with your pet supplier as to the appropriateness of each product.

albumins, globulins and protamines, all of which are basic building ingredients of the living cells. Proteins are not only concerned with the growth, repair and replacement of body tissues; particular kinds of proteins are responsible for various metabolic functions and include enzymes, antibodies and hormones. Proteins are important to the digestion; without them the system would not be able to convert

the inner seed from the husk, seeds probably forming more than 90% of the diet of these little birds. Let us have a brief look at the basic dietary constituents and discuss their individual merits.

Proteins: These are made up from chains of amino acids and are essential to the structure and function of all living organisms. Proteins may consist of many different amino acids, each forming structural substances such as

ingested foods into the essential dietary constituents. The main source of proteins for Zebra Finches is the various seeds that are fed to them.

Carbohydrates: These can be divided into two main groups: the sugars (monosaccharides and disaccharides) and the starches (polysaccharides), all of which are important in producing energy and thus body heat. The main part of a

Feeding

Zebra Finch's diet should consist of carbohydrates, as these little birds are full of boundless energy. Carbohydrates are found in almost every item of food eaten by them.

Fats: These help to keep the birds warm and act as a food reserve should times become

Vitamins: While proteins, carbohydrates and fats are required in large amounts in the diet and are considered to be *macronutrients*, vitamins and minerals *(micronutrients)* are required in minute quantities. In spite of this, however, the importance of vitamins should not be underestimated. Vitamin A

Provide a variety of seed dishes which are kept filled with various seeds and grit. Grit is an important digestive aid for a bird and should be available daily.

difficult or should extra energy be required at any time. Fats may be ingested directly from oils contained in the seed, or excess carbohydrates may be converted into them. Fat cells are stored in the subcutaneous tissue and act as an insulator against heat loss; they also represent a considerable energy source in times of adversity. Fat may also act as a shock-absorbing tissue. Excessive aggregations of fat cells cause obesity, so a certain amount of care should be taken in the selection of seeds given to the birds.

helps in the fight against diseases, particularly those of the respiratory tract. The vitamin-B complex promotes healthy growth, assists in the function of the nerves and enhances the condition of the plumage, as well as increases the efficiency of the digestive system. Vitamin C is thought to be unnecessary to birds. Vitamin D is important to the growth and repair of bone; lack of it in young birds can lead to rickets.

Vitamin E is important for muscular co-ordination, and a lack of it in the gravid hen will lead to abnormal development in the embryos.

Minerals: A number of mineral salts are required to add the so-called trace elements to the diet; most of these are contained in sufficient quantities in the normal food. Calcium and phosphorus however, in conjunction with vitamin D, are important in bone formation, the prevention of rickets and, in particular, the formation of the egg shell in gravid hens. Both vitamins and minerals can be provided in a supplementary form, and it is possible to purchase several makes of excellent multivitamin–mineral preparations from your pharmacist, veterinarian or pet shop. Such preparations may be obtained in powder or fluid form; the former can be added to the seed, the latter to the drinking water in quantities recommended by the manufacturer. It is not easy to give an overdose of vitamins or minerals, but one should work in "pinches" or "drops" rather than larger quantities.

Another important source of minerals is the grit which is given to the birds to help them digest their food. Specially prepared grit for birds usually includes insoluble and soluble parts. The insoluble parts of the grit remain in the bird's gizzard; when it mixes with the ingested food, the muscular walls of the gizzard expand and contract, grinding up the seed until it is a digestible paste, before it is passed into the duodenum for further digestion. The soluble grit (which is present in much smaller amounts) contains such trace elements as

calcium, phosphorus, iodine, sodium, sulphur, potassium, iron, copper, cobalt and many others in minute quantities.

The most important mineral is calcium; this may be given in addition to grit, mineral supplements or mineral blocks. One good source of calcium is cuttlefish bone, which may be given crushed or in a solid piece; one can purchase a special holder for cuttlefish bone which can be clipped to the wire of the cage or aviary. An advantage of solid cuttlefish bone is that it will give the birds some exercise and help to keep their beaks in good condition as they peck out the pieces.

Nesting finches will consume greater amounts of cuttlefish bone, however this calcium source is necessary for continued good health in all birds.

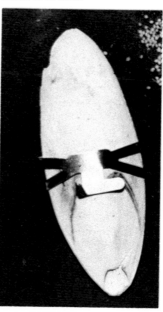

Feeding

Cuttlefish bone may be purchased from your petshop or, if you are lucky enough to live near the seashore, you may be able to collect your own. In the latter case, the bone should be allowed to soak in clear running water for at least twenty-four hours and then dried out before being given to the birds—this is to remove excessive sodium chloride.

Fresh water is best supplied through one of the many commercially available drinking fonts.

Water: Although it may seem obvious that the birds require water at all times, a few words about this essential commodity will not go amiss. It is said that water forms more than 90% of all living organisms and, if you were able to remove all of the water from any animal or bird, you would be left with a little pile of dust. Without water, all of the other ingredients of the balanced diet would be useless. Water forms the greater part of the blood, which transports nutrients in solution about the body; it is required to keep the internal organs lubricated, and it acts as a cooling agent when hot conditions prevail.

Tap water is quite all right for your birds, as is rainwater or well water; if we can drink it, it will be safe for the birds. Drinking fonts are the best way of offering drinking water to your birds. They usually hold a fair amount and have a small drinking aperture which keeps the water unpolluted for longer than it would be in an open vessel. Water in drinking fonts should be changed daily, and the font should be cleaned out with a brush at least once per week. In the aviary, your birds will probably have a bath or pond. They will most certainly drink from this, which is not bad, providing the water is changed regularly and the container kept spotless.

Seed
The biggest part of the wild Zebra Finch's diet consists of the seeds of grasses and other plants. As a supplement, the birds will eat greenfood and perhaps a little insect food; for their mineral supplies they will swallow small pieces of grit and earth. Zebra Finches are easy to feed in captivity, and the seed we can buy will contain all of

the macronutrients we have already mentioned. However, as already discussed, it will be necessary to give them a supplement of micronutrients.

Most pet shops and avicultural suppliers also sell so-called finch mixtures, consisting mainly of millet, canary seed, oats, niger, rape and perhaps others. If you have a large number of birds, purchasing seed in this way is usually uneconomical, and you are best advised to purchase the different seeds in greater bulk and make your own mixtures. Another advantage of doing this is that you can vary the mixtures according to the season and the requirements of your birds.

The main constituent of food for Zebra Finches should be millet, of which there are several kinds; it may be worth

experimenting with small quantities of different millets to see which your birds prefer. The different sorts will vary in size or color, but their nutritional values are similar. Millet seeds are globular and average 2mm in diameter; the color ranges through various shades of straw yellow. Most of the color in the millet is in the husk, which is discarded by the bird before it eats the kernel, so the color is not important. Millet is an excellent basic diet, containing a great deal of energy-giving carbohydrate. However, as it is low in proteins and fats, it is necessary to provide your birds with additional seeds to boost these nutrients. The second main ingredient is canary seed, which has a significantly greater protein and fat content. Small quantities of other seeds, such as niger and rape, can be added to increase the content of protein and fat. A good general mixture would

A well-rounded diet will include fresh growing greens.

Feeding

consist of 60% mixed millets, 30% canary seed, 5% niger and 5% rape. As an occasional change, other seeds such as sesame, caraway, poppy, fennel or hemp may be given in small quantities. The oily seeds may be increased by a few per cent in the breeding season, and the millet and canary reduced appropriately. The accompanying table gives a general guide to the nutritional content of the various foodstuffs offered to Zebra Finches. The percentages are of course variable, depending on the quality of the seeds, but they do express a reasonable average of what may be expected.

replenish the seed and clean the containers without disturbing the inmates. In an aviary, it is best to place the seed dishes in the shelter. A small shelf can be rigged up at a convenient height and a

Seed hoppers deliver a steady supply of seed.

Nutritional Composition of Seeds (in percentages)

Seed	Protein	Carbohydrate	Fat	Fiber	Minerals
Millet	14	65	2	8	4
Canary seed	16	30	5	20	4
Hemp	16	25	30	18	6
Niger	19	12	42	14	3
Rape	21	19	43	7	4
Sesame	20	20	47	6	6
Caraway	20	30	17	12	7
Poppy	22	10	48	5	7
Fennel	17	32	12	15	8

Feed Containers

Mixtures of dried seeds are best placed in seed dispensers or flat dishes, which are preferably raised on platforms above the aviary floor. In cages, special plastic seed containers are available which can be clipped to the wire front, enabling you to

sliding door can be placed in the wire mesh, so that these can be serviced without entering the shelter.

As Zebra Finches remove the husks from the seeds before swallowing the kernels, it is obvious that the bulk of the husks will fall back into the seed pots. If you do not keep an eye on this, a thick layer of husks will form over the untouched seed, and the birds will begin to starve. The husks are very light and can easily be removed by blowing gently across the surface of the food container. If you have large numbers of birds, it may well be worth investing in a winnowing machine, which will separate the husks from the good seed and can save you a lot of money. Inspect the feed containers twice each day, removing husks and replacing seed as necessary.

Larger seed hoppers are better suited for aviaries.

Millet Sprays

For some reason or other Zebra Finches (and other seed-eating birds) love to remove the seeds from their natural stems. Millet sprays

Spray millet is commercially available and delights most Zebra Finches. In aviaries several sprays can be hung in bunches.

are available which consist of the seeds attached to their original stems. These may be obtained from your pet shop and are more expensive than normal millet seed, but the birds love them and gain exercise while clinging to the sprays and pecking out the

seed. There is also some evidence that spray millet is slightly more nutritious than thrashed seed. Millet sprays can be tied up in bundles of three or four stems and hung up on the cage or aviary wire. Alternatively, they may be placed upright in a vase or bottle which has been sunk into the ground or weighted down to keep it from over-balancing.

Soaked Seed

As a change, and especially during the breeding season or during the periodic molt, your birds can be given seed which has been soaked in water. Prepare only enough seed

The germination of seed increases its protein and vitamin content and supplies greater nutrition to the birds.

which can be used immediately, as it quickly sours and could upset your birds' digestive system if you are not careful. Take a quantity of your usual seed mixture, place it in a container and add cold water until the seed is waterlogged. Leave it to stand in a warm place (perhaps the airing cupboard) for a period of twenty-four hours, then rinse it off with clean, cold water through a strainer, shaking out the excess moisture. The soaked seed is then placed in a dish and given to the birds. Not only do the birds love this change, but it is extremely good for them. As the seed is soaking, the various processes which cause it to germinate will begin. During germination the biochemical composition of the seed will

change; the protein content increases and the levels of B-complex vitamins rise—a useful addition to the diet, especially during the breeding season. Millet sprays can be soaked and hung up in the same way. Soaked seed should never be left in the

Romaine lettuce and other garden vegetables can be offered to the birds.

Greenfood

This is a very useful source of nutrients for Zebra Finches, as it contains a range of proteins, vitamins and minerals and helps to correct any dietary deficiencies which may occur in birds receiving a seed diet exclusively. Greenfood in the diet reduces the risk of obesity arising from too many oily seeds. Seeding grasses are a particularly appreciated addition to a

cage or aviary for more than twenty-four hours, as it will go sour. Try to feed an amount which can be quickly consumed; any left the following day should be discarded and replaced with fresh soaked seed.

captive Zebra Finch's diet, and you can actually allow these to grow in your outside flight where the birds will forage among the foliage. In addition, you can collect seeding grass heads from wild areas in the

Zebras will derive the benefits of grit and trace minerals from grass sod.

neighborhood, being sure that you avoid material which has been polluted by pesticides, herbicides, fungicides or traffic fumes. Other items which will be enjoyed by your birds are chickweed, groundsel, dandelion, thistle heads, lettuce, spinach and plantain. All should be given fresh and removed as soon as they start to wilt. It is possible to keep certain greenfoods fresh by inserting them in water, just as one would treat a vase of flowers, but ensuring that there are no cavities left into which the birds could fall and drown.

Greenfood should be fed regularly in small quantities, rather than large amounts now and again, as this could disturb the digestive processes. Too much greenfood may cause diarrhea, although the birds are usually sensible enough to know when they have had too much of a particular thing. During the breeding season, the amount of greenfood may be increased, although some breeders advocate it being given early in the day only, thus ensuring that the youngsters' crops are filled with seed before settling down for the night, rather than greenfood which is less substantial. Some Zebra Finches will appreciate fruits, such as apples, pears or grapes, which are cut in half and impaled on a twig, allowing the birds to peck out pieces at random.

Additional Foods

Although Zebra Finches will do very well and breed satisfactorily given a range of the foodstuffs already described, they will enjoy receiving the occasional treat, and you will enjoy giving it to

A variety of foods are appreciated. Offer scrambled eggs with the egg shells left in the mixture as an added source of calcium.

them. First of all, bear in mind that a treat is a treat only, and remember that too much of what we like is almost always bad for us. The same goes for the birds; when giving them treats, make sure it is in sensible quantities. The following are a number of ideas; some birds will like them, others will not, and there is nothing to prevent you from experimenting with your own ideas: stale sponge cake mixed with a little warm milk and honey, stale wholemeal bread soaked in water and squeezed dry, cream cheese on toast, mashed banana, dates, boiled potato, boiled rice (even rice pudding) and many, many more.

Breeding

Zebra Finches are one of the easiest of aviary birds to breed. All you need to do is to place a pair together in a cage or aviary, give them facilities to nest, and they will soon be rearing a clutch. However, this does not mean that it is easy to breed specimens of exhibition quality; some of the expensive than the average, but will be well worth it. It is preferable to obtain young birds from the current year's broods, rather than to purchase older stock of dubious age. Zebra Finches may be purchased from the pet shop, from the avicultural supplier or direct from the

A Normal female Zebra finch in a nest of twigs.

top breeders may have taken years and many generations of birds to reach the standards required to win prizes on the show bench.

Acquiring Stock

If you intend to produce good show birds eventually, you are best advised to purchase stock from a proven strain. Such birds will be a little more breeder. When entering an establishment to purchase birds, it is always a good idea to give a cursory inspection of the premises. Ensure that the birds are kept in the kinds of conditions in which you would expect to keep your own. Signs that the birds are being kept in unhealthy conditions will include dark, dingy, unventilated premises; untidy cages; buildup of droppings on floors, walls and perches; dirty food pots and water containers; and, of course, sickness in the birds themselves. However excited you may be about making your first acquisitions, such premises should be avoided at all cost unless you want to be troubled with sickness in your birds. Find another supplier who takes pride in the display of his surplus birds; you will soon learn to distinguish between the good and the bad propositions.

Another point about purchasing from a successful breeder is that his stock will have been kept in the best possible conditions—if not, he would never have been successful on the show bench. Wherever you purchase your birds, there are a few points to consider before making a decision. You will want to avoid obtaining unhealthy stock, but remember that most breeders and dealers will be very reluctant to reimburse you for birds which are found to be ailing *after* they have left their premises. One can hardly blame them for this; how are they to know the kind of stress a bird may go through once it is out of their care?

Healthy young birds (indeed, older ones as well) should be alert and lively, moving readily from perch to perch when approached and frequently making their cheeping call. The eyes should be bright and free of discharge, and the plumage should be sleek, tight and clean, particularly in the area around the vent. Birds which

A pair of Zebra Finches will share the responsibility of egg incubation.

47

Breeding

sit hunched up in a corner, with their feathers fluffed out, their eyes partly closed and showing little interest in what is going on around them, should be refused.

If possible, try to handle the bird before it is purchased. If they are in a stock cage, they may be caught in the hand; in an aviary a padded net should

Also of the Fawn color is this Fawn Black-breasted female.

be used. The bird is gently but firmly held in the palm of the hand belly upwards, with the head restrained *extremely gently* between two of the fingers. It is then easy to feel the breast with the fingers of the other hand. The flesh

should be plump and firm, and there should be no hollows on either side of the breastbone. Finally, if you intend to breed a particular color variety, you will want to select those birds as near as possible to the standard for that variety.

Sexing

If you intend to breed Zebra Finches, it is obvious that you will require to know how the two sexes are distinguished. Differences in color or form in animals are known as *sexual dimorphism* and are quite obvious in normal Zebra Finches and most of the varieties. Even in varieties such as the Whites, where the color difference between cock and hen is not obvious, the beak of the latter is usually paler in color. In some difficult cases, they can only be sexed by studying the behavior (i.e., a bird displaying to another bird is usually a cock). In general, the cock possesses an orange patch on each cheek and a white spotted chestnut patch along each flank; both of these features are absent from the hen.

Colony Breeding

Some breeders like to allow groups of birds in an aviary to breed on the colony system. You are unlikely to produce any prize winners using this method, but the offspring will be average healthy birds, some of which may be of sufficiently high standard to use in your selective breeding later on. Birds introduced in an aviary should be in equal numbers of cocks and hens and, particularly if there are a number of birds strange to each other, they should preferably be introduced all at the same time. This way, they will all be in a strange new territory together and will be too busy exploring and making new friends to worry about bullying. Cocks and hens will soon pair up and go to nest if you have provided them with nesting sites.

In outdoor aviaries, it is advisable not to allow your birds to nest until late spring at least, as excessively cold weather can lead to egg binding in the hens, failure of eggs to hatch or casualties in the young. Zebra Finches are not seasonal breeders and will go to nest at any time if they have nest boxes. To prevent them from breeding, the answer is to deny them the nesting sites until you are ready to supply them.

Nest Boxes

Zebra Finches are not at all fussy as to the type of nest box you supply them; indeed, some of them may not use a nest box at all and may construct a nest in a surprising and unintended spot in the aviary. The author recalls constructing his first aviary, the shelter of which had a rather ambitious "Alpine villa" roof. The eaves of the roof overhung into the flight, and the Zebra Finches immediately took the space

The male Fawn Black-breasted Zebra Finch is diversely colored from the female.

under the eaves to have been made specially for them to nest in! In this case, the nest boxes were totally ignored, and four pairs of birds reared several broods under the eaves. The lesson here is, if you want to control the nesting habits of your birds, you must ensure that there are no potential nest sites in the aviary other than those which you have provided.

The usual types of nesting containers for Zebra Finches are either boxes or baskets. The former should be about 15cm (6in) cubed, with a removable top and a half-open front. You can purchase

Many forms of nesting containers are available, besides the more conventional wooden nest boxes.

these boxes in your pet shop, or they are quite easy to make, using 6mm (¼ in) plywood, pinned and glued together. Wickerwork baskets are also eagerly accepted, these being globular in structure and about 15cm (6in) in diameter, with a large entrance hole in the front. Whether using boxes or baskets, or a mixture of the two, you should allow two sites for each pair of birds, to help prevent squabbling over a particular site by giving a wider choice. The nesting containers should be placed within the aviary shelter or in a sheltered part of the flight, preferably all at the same height, again designed to prevent squabbling for the highest spot.

Each nesting container should be half filled with nesting material which is roughly fashioned into the shape of a nest; the birds will soon take over and build a nest to their own specifications. Nesting material can consist of bundles of clean hay, raffia, horsehair and pieces of wool from unravelled garments. The birds will also use some of their own fallen feathers for lining the nest. Additional material should be placed in bundles about the aviary, and the birds will select what they require. As soon as the birds begin to lay, the excess nesting material should be removed, as Zebra Finches, being such zealous builders, have a habit of continuing to add to the nest while brooding. In severe cases, two or three clutches of eggs will be covered completely with nesting material, creating the so-called egg sandwiches, in which most of the eggs will never hatch.

Selective Breeding
Colony breeding in the aviary has its good points; in a flight the birds make an attractive display, particularly if you

keep a range of color varieties. You will also be able to study the communal behavior of the birds as they go about their daily business. To produce good show specimens, however, you must keep your pairs separately in suitable breeding cages. A good size for such a breeding cage is 60cm long × 37.5cm high × 37.5cm deep (24in x 15in x

Wicker baskets have been widely used in the breeding of Zebra Finches.

variety, should be chosen. (Although Zebra Finches will breed as early as three months of age, greater success can be expected from birds of six months or more.) In some cases, it will be necessary to mate two different varieties together in order to improve certain aspects of one or the other. The cages are prepared, complete with a nest box rigged up, usually in one of the rear corners of the cage, before the birds are introduced.

15in). It is a good idea to build the cages in pairs, divided by a sliding panel which can be removed to give an extra long flight, should you need extra space for young stock.

The pairs are selected for their individual attributes, and only healthy, robust specimens, with good markings for the selected

Mating

As soon as the birds are in breeding condition, the cock will begin to display to the hen by fluttering his wings, spreading his tail and uttering his comical little song. In the initial stages the hen will usually ignore the apparent madness in the male and will go nonchalantly about her business. Soon she will start collecting nesting material, making a large, untidy nest in the nest box. As soon as the nest is well underway, the hen will succumb to the attentions of the amorous male and allow him to mate with her. To accomplish this, the cock has to balance himself precariously on the hen's back and bring his tail under hers so that their respective vents are in apposition to each other. This appears to be a difficult task for the birds, and it is essential that they be supplied with secure, robust perches, so that they do not fall off each time mating is attempted. It may take a few attempts for a successful mating, bearing in mind that in most birds, fertilization is external in that the sperm is literally sprayed at the vent of the hen by the cock. A single, successful mating, however, will ensure that all eggs in a particular clutch are fertile.

Selective breeding, on a large scale, can best be accomplished through the use of separate breeding cages.

Brooding

The hen will begin to spend longer periods in the nest prior to laying, and it is essential that she has access to calcium supplements such as cuttlefish bone at this time, so that the egg shells can be properly formed. It is also a good idea to feed additional greenfood and "tonic" foods during the whole of the breeding period. The eggs are white in color and about 12mm (½ in) in length; they are very fragile, and if it should be necessary to handle them, this should be done with great care. The average number in the clutch is five or six, but may be as few as three or as many as ten. Incubation may not start immediately on the laying of the first egg, so it is possible that two or three chicks may hatch at the same time. Both the cock and the hen share in the incubation of the eggs and will usually spend the nights in the nest box together.

Fertility

Being quite prolific, Zebra Finches rarely have problems of infertility, but occasional failures to hatch can be caused by one of two reasons; either fertilization was unsuccessful in the first place, or the embryos have died in the shell at a certain stage of their development. In the former case, failure to successfully fertilize the eggs can be a fault in either sex. The mating of young, inexperienced birds can lead to infertility, as can attempting to breed when the weather is too cold. Inadequate diet can also be problematic. It is best not to attempt breeding Zebras until they are at least six, preferably nine months of age. If you ensure that they are properly fed and cared for, as already discussed, the problems of infertility will be minimized.

Some breeders like to check the eggs of all their birds for fertility during the early days of the brooding, so that time will not be wasted with birds sitting on infertile eggs. If examined in front of a strong light, a fertile egg which has been brooded for three days or more will show a network of red blood vessels just below the surface of the shell, indicating that the embryo has begun to develop. As the embryo grows, the egg will become opaque, and a dark shadow will be discernible. A useful piece of apparatus to have is a so-called egg candler; this consists of an enclosed box which contains a light bulb connected to the electric line or a powerful battery. By holding the egg in front of a small hole in one side of the box, a concentrated beam of

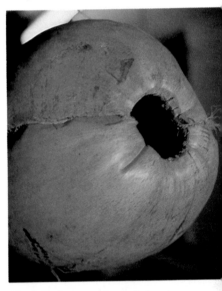

The hull of a coconut recycled as a nesting container.

light will illuminate the interior of the shell, enabling one to easily ascertain if embryonic development is taking place. An infertile egg, which is sometimes referred to as a "clear" egg, will, of course, always appear translucent, with no embryonic shadow or blood vessels apparent.

A pair of Zebras which produce a clutch of infertile eggs should be separated and each kept with members of its own sex for a week or so, before attempting another pairing with different mates. This is another advantage of breeding pairs separately in cages; such action would be extremely difficult, if not impossible, with birds breeding on the colony system. Zebras are usually quite accommodating when it comes to inspecting their nests, eggs or young, although such inspections should be carried out

The incubation period for Zebra Finch eggs is ten days.

infrequently and preferably when both birds are away from the nest feeding. It is a good idea to offer greenfood or soaked millet spray immediately prior to a nest inspection, so as to lure the brooding birds away from the nest for a few minutes. Birds which persistently lay infertile

clutches should no longer be used for breeding attempts and should perhaps be relegated to the ornamental flight.

If eggs which were obviously fertile fail to hatch within fourteen days, death in the shell must be suspected. Fortunately, this does not occur often, but it may be attributed to inadequate humidity in the nesting environment, inadequate diet in the hen during egg development, or too much disturbance during the brooding. Inadequate humidity rarely occurs in nests in outdoor aviaries but may be a problem in breeding cages. In excessively dry conditions, it is recommended that the interior and surroundings of the cages be finely sprayed with water. Birds breeding in cages are also more prone to disturbances, and it is a good idea to cover part of the cage front with a piece of translucent plastic, which will give the nesting birds a greater sense of security without reducing the light intensity inside the cage too dramatically.

Rearing

The period of incubation is about ten days, although the first chicks are not likely to appear until twelve days after the first egg is laid, as serious incubation does not normally commence until the second or third egg has been laid. The newly hatched chicks are tiny and naked, with their eyes firmly sealed. The cock and the hen will share in feeding the young, regurgitating seed and greenfood. It is most important at this time to make soaked seed and greenfood available if the rearing is to be successful. Some avicultural suppliers provide special rearing foods to be given to the adults at this time; although it is not strictly essential to give this to your birds, it will certainly do no harm and will perhaps improve your chances of getting strong specimens. The nestlings will grow rapidly and, in a few days, the eyes will open and the plumage begin to form.

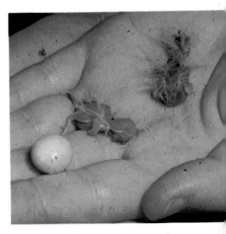

Two- and one-day-old Zebra Finch chicks, with an egg about to hatch.

Fledging

By the fifteenth day, the nestlings will be fully feathered and beginning to show an interest in the outside world. They will sit near the edge of the nest box opening and struggle for the most advantageous position when the parents come with food. By the eighteenth day, the youngsters will have left the nest and will be making their first amateurish attempts to fly; they learn quickly however, and within twenty-four hours they will be flying about as well as the adults. The parents will continue to feed the youngsters for about ten days after they have left the nest, until they have learned to feed themselves. A close watch should be kept on the birds at this time, because if the parents want to go to nest again, they are likely to attack the original brood as soon as the chicks become independent.

Newly independent youngsters, especially those in breeding cages, should be moved to stock accommodation as soon as possible. It is rather difficult to distinguish the sexes of young Zebras until they are about eight weeks old; they are all similar in color to an adult hen, and the beaks are brownish black. At ten weeks, the markings of the adult cock will have begun to appear, but before this occurs only a rough idea of the sexes can be ascertained by looking at the beak color as it changes to deep coral red in the cock and a lighter orange red in the hen.

As soon as the sexes are apparent, it is desirable to separate them, especially if they are in a community aviary

A male Crested Zebra Finch guarding his nest of week old hatchlings.

with nest boxes; otherwise they are likely to mate prematurely and make a hash of their nesting attempts.

Ringing

Most serious breeders of Zebra Finches like to keep records of their birds' breeding accomplishments. Each bird is given a number and a record of its history is kept either on stock cards or in a stud book. Such cards or books may be purchased from publishers or avicultural

suppliers or from societies. These are already printed with appropriate headings and spaces to fill in the information. It is all very well giving each bird a number, but with a quantity of specimens, many of which will bear great resemblance to each other, how are we to distinguish which is which? This is done by ringing, which is the application of a numbered or colored ring, or band, to the bird's leg. If you buy your initial stock from an established breeder, the birds are most likely to be already banded. One can then start with these numbers as a basis for one's own ringing system, which will develop as breeding progresses.

There are two methods of ringing. The first is known as the "split ring" method. Split rings are usually made of plastic and come in a variety of colors; they are often used without numbers, and identification of the birds is accomplished by color coding. Such rings are useful for temporary identification,

Special attention must be paid to the diet of the parenting Zebra Finches.

with the year of issue. As close ringing can only be carried out on nestling birds, it gives a reliable indication of age. The rings are also stamped with individual numbers, thus simplifying the keeping of records. Hints on how to ring young Zebra Finches may be obtained from the supplier of the rings, but it is important to ring the chicks at the correct age; if the bird is too young, the ring will either slip off or become fixed higher up the leg than was intended, resulting in possible damage to the limb; if the

as they can be applied to the leg of a bird of any age, using a special tool.

The more reliable and official method however, is known as "close ringing." Many avicultural societies supply official rings made of metal, which are stamped

chick is too old, it will be impossible to get the ring on at all. Zebra Finches are usually ready to be close-ringed between eight and ten days of age. Experience will teach you how to recognize the appropriate time. It is a good idea for beginners to

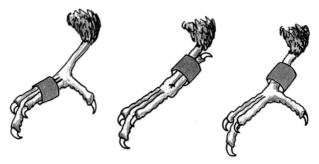

Zebra finches between eight and ten days old are ready to be close-ringed.

watch more experienced fanciers ringing their birds before attempting it themselves. It is best to try and ring the chicks when the parents are absent from the nest and to do it as quickly as possible, with the minimum of fuss. It may be more convenient for a right-handed person to hold the chick in the left hand, with the leg to be

An eight-day-old chick awaiting food from its parent.

ringed held between the thumb and forefinger. The three forward-pointing toes are gathered together and the ring is passed over them, sliding past the fourth toe which is parallel to the leg. The ring should then sit comfortably on the lower leg, held in position by the toes when they are respread.

Fostering

It is not often necessary to foster Zebra chicks, but, fortunately, most pairs will accept extra chicks readily, providing they are of similar

size and age. Sometimes a pair will have an excessively large clutch of eight or more, while another pair will only have two or three. In such cases it may be wise to share out the clutches of eggs or chicks so that each pair has a similar quantity to rear. Sometimes one of the parent successful. In such instances, it is advisable to foster out most of the chicks if possible, although one or two can be left with the single parent to keep it happy. One problem which arises with fostering is identification of the nestlings. If eggs are fostered out to a pair which already have eggs

Fawn chicks a few days apart in age.

birds may die or become incapacitated and, while both cock and hen are dedicated parents and will attempt to hatch and rear a clutch on their own, this will put a lot of strain on the individual, which is likely to be only partially of their own, it will be impossible to tell which is which when they hatch, unless they are of totally different varieties. Of course, if chicks are fostered out *after* they have been close-ringed, the problem will be solved, but sometimes it will be a case either of difficulty in identification or of losing a clutch altogether.

Health

Health in any animal may be defined as the degree of absence of disease, and an animal in good health will be free of all disease and have soundness of the body, with all organs functioning correctly. Such a state will manifest itself in a general zest for life which will be apparent in the demeanor. To maintain good health in our Zebra Finches, stringent practices of hygiene are necessary; this may sound water, and ensures that they are not subjected to periods of stress—then ill health is unlikely to become a problem. Hygiene is the science of prevention of disease, and prevention is infinitely better than cure, as well as being easier. Although Zebra Finches are one of the hardiest species in cage or aviary, they will succumb to neglect, just as any of the less robust species will, although they will perhaps take a little

The skeletal anatomy of a finch: the bones of the limbs are colored blue.

complicated but really is nothing more than following the procedures already discussed in housing and feeding. As long as one starts with healthy birds, provides them with draftfree and damp-proof, clean accommodation, gives them a balanced diet of grit, greenfood and fresh longer. However, even in the most hygienic of establishments, the occasional accident or outbreak of disease may occur, and it is wise to know how to prevent or treat such cases.

Quarantine

If you have existing stock, it is always dangerous to introduce new birds which you have obtained elsewhere before allowing a quarantine period of at least 14 days. The bird or birds you have obtained may have come from reliable premises and may have appeared to be in the appears in the fourteen-day period, you can be assured that it is only healthy birds which you are introducing to your existing stock.

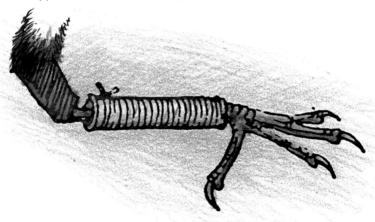

Suspected leg breaks can be bandaged until they can be checked by a veterinarian.

best of health, but there is always the remote chance that an infection is present which has not advanced enough to display any symptoms. The purpose of quarantine therefore is to keep new birds separate from existing stock, to ascertain that they are free from disease which could otherwise infect all of your birds, with disastrous consequences. It is best to keep a special quarantine cage or aviary in a separate room or outhouse, well away from the other stock. Any new birds should be placed in quarantine and observed daily for signs or symptoms of trouble. If nothing untoward

Accidental Injuries

Accidental injuries, such as broken bones or wounds, are not only unpleasant in themselves but can cause stress in the birds which will reduce resistance to disease and render them susceptible to infection. Broken bones can result from the birds flying into unprotected glass windows in bird rooms, or as a result of being shocked at night by vermin or predators. Broken wings or legs can often be set by a veterinarian, using a splint and plaster, but such breakages rarely heal perfectly; unless the bird is a particularly valuable breeding specimen, it is perhaps best to have it euthanized.

Open wounds are rare in Zebra Finches but may be caused by the birds getting caught in loose wire netting (one reason for regular inspection of your cages and aviaries) or possibly from fighting or bullying, especially from birds of other species which may share the accommodation. In severe cases, a veterinarian should be consulted, who may decide to suture the wound and apply a dressing. In minor cases, the application of a mild antiseptic cream and isolation in a quiet, warm cage will usually result in healing within a few days.

Claws should never be allowed to become this grossly overgrown. Clip claws when necessary with sharp nail clippers.

Overgrown Claws

Providing Zebra Finches are given adequate exercise space, various-sized perches (including natural twigs) and a supply of sand or sandpaper on the floor, problems with overgrown claws are unlikely to develop. In rare cases, however, the claws may grow longer than is naturally acceptable, and the birds will have problems in perching. It is quite easy to trim the claws, using a pair of sharp nail clippers or scissors. The bird should be grasped gently in the hand and its toes manipulated with the thumb and forefinger. If the nails are held up in front of a strong light, the blood vessel, or quick, can be seen. The nail should be sheared off about 3mm (1/8in) below the blood vessel, care being taken not to sever the vessel itself, which will bleed profusely. In accidental cases of bleeding, a styptic pencil or a solution of alum should be applied to the wound to stem the flow of blood. Overgrown beaks occur even less frequently, but cases of the upper or lower mandible outgrowing the other will make it increasingly difficult for the bird to feed, and it will eventually die of starvation if not treated. The clipping of a bird's beak is a somewhat delicate operation and one is advised to consult a veterinarian or experienced aviculturist before making a first attempt. The beak is also supplied with blood, so great care must be taken.

The Hospital Cage

Many bird diseases and conditions can be treated by placing the bird in a warm environment. The serious keeper of Zebra Finches would be wise to have a hospital cage in which to isolate and treat any birds which succumb to sickness. A hospital cage may be purchased or made; it need not be very big, 45cm long × 30cm deep × 45cm high (18in × 12in × 18in) would be adequate. The cage contains a thermostatically controlled heater which may be adjusted to various temperatures. The heater is normally set below a wire grid in the base of the cage, and a number of ventilation holes in the upper part of the sides and back will help create a rising convection current of warm air. A single perch is set fairly low down in the cage and, of course, the usual food and water dishes must be provided. The hospital cage can be used for birds with a number of ailments, including egg-binding, respiratory infections, digestive disorders and even those recovering from accidental injuries. A temperature of 29°–32°C (85°–90°F) should be set on the thermostat when the sick bird is introduced, and this should be maintained constantly during the period of sickness. The adjustable thermostat is important because, when the bird has recovered, it will be necessary to gradually reduce the temperature over a number of days, to acclimatize the bird back to room temperature. Birds which have come from outside aviaries should not be returned outside until they have spent a month indoors or, if it is during the winter, they should not be put outside until the following late spring.

A male Pied Fawn Zebra Finch.

Stress

Stress in captive birds may be described as a state of prolonged shock which may be caused by a number of factors. Stress is a mental condition which puts a strain on the metabolism of the body functions and can reduce the normal resistance to pathogenic diseases. Birds which have been recently captured from the wild are most susceptible to stress, as they are suffering from the trauma of being caught and then confined in a small space. It is an unfortunate fact that a high percentage of birds caught in the wild for avicultural purposes rarely survive for more than a few days, which is why those that make it to their final destinations usually command high prices. Fortunately, pressure from humane and conservation groups in the last few years has led to many countries banning the export of certain species, and legislation to improve the transport husbandry of others has led to great improvements in the health of imported birds.

An assortment of perches, in different sizes and grades, will help in maintaining short claws.

Due to the fact that the vast majority of captive Zebra Finches have been bred in cages and aviaries for generations, they are not quite so susceptible to stress as are many other birds. However, stress can and does occur, and we should do all in our power to keep it to the minimum. Great care should be taken in catching up birds, handling them, transporting them and settling them. Stress can be caused by cold, damp or drafty accommodation. Continual frights will also place a great strain on the birds, and cages or aviaries should always be approached slowly and purposefully, with no sudden or surprising movements. Children and pets can be a problem if they continually run toward the cage or aviary— they must be prevented from doing so. Disturbance at night is another factor which causes stress and, once settled in the evening, the birds should never be disturbed except in a case of emergency. Prowling cats or vermin can be a problem at night, and every effort should be made to discourage the former and eradicate the latter.

Egg Binding

This is a problem which may occasionally occur in gravid hens, resulting from an egg or eggs becoming lodged in the oviduct. The condition is potentially fatal; it requires immediate treatment should it be diagnosed. Birds suffering from stress due to factors such as chilling are susceptible to egg binding, as are those receiving an inadequate diet. Lack of

calcium is an important contributing factor to egg binding, and breeding birds must always have access to cuttlefish bone and mineral supplements. Immature birds are also likely to suffer.

If a breeding hen appears to be unwell, egg binding should be the first condition suspected. Suffering birds will usually sit fluffed up

Birds breeding in colder seasons are more susceptible to egg binding. If this afflication is suspected, heat treatments should begin immediately.

unsteadily on a perch and will have lost their desire to go about nest-tidying activities. The sick bird should be immediately removed to a hospital cage and maintained at a temperature of about 30°C (85°F). In most cases, such heat treatment will suffice to allow the egg to be successfully voided. In severe cases however, in which the egg is not voided after eight hours under heat treatment, an application of a suitable lubricant such as castor oil to the vent may help. Any persistent cases should be referred to a veterinarian, who may attempt to effect a cure by an injection; such severe cases, however, are usually fatal. Birds which recover satisfactorily should not be used for breeding again during the season.

A Fawn Zebra male; insert shows a female variant that has a yellow bill.

Digestive Problems

There are a number of disorders affecting the digestive system, most of which are caused by an invasion of pathogenic organisms in the bowel. Diarrhea, manifesting itself in loose, watery droppings, is often a symptom of such infections and is accompanied by a dirty, wet area around the vent. Digestive problems are not common in Zebra Finches kept in clean conditions, but food soiled by the excrement of infected (wild) birds or rodents is a common source of infection. Scrupulous cleanliness of food and water dispensers should be maintained and attempts made to keep vermin away from the aviary.

In addition to diarrhea, sick birds will show the usual signs of sickness or fever, sitting fluffed up in some corner and showing little interest in what is going on; in some cases, vomiting and a craving for grit will be apparent. All such symptoms must be viewed with concern because, while the sickness may be nothing more than a mild attack of enteritis, there is the possibility that a more serious infectious disease such as coccidiosis may be involved. Your veterinarian may be able to diagnose the disease from fecal or blood samples (in cases of death, from a necropsy) and recommend the course of action to take. Luckily, many enteric diseases will respond to treatment with antibiotics. Sick birds should be placed in isolation in a hospital cage and treated as recommended.

Respiratory Problems

These occur most usually in birds accommodated in damp or overcrowded conditions, or in poorly ventilated rooms. The organisms responsible for respiratory infections are present in the air most of the time, but in varying quantities. Normal healthy birds possess a built-in resistance to most of these organisms, but stress caused by unhealthy conditions can reduce resistance, and an infection can break out. Symptoms of respiratory problems include a thick nasal discharge coupled with an obvious difficulty in breathing and the usual hunched-up appearance of a fevered bird.

There are several kinds of respiratory infections which may be caused by any of an assortment of organisms and which vary in severity. Conditions similar to the common cold or sinusitis can usually be cured by placing the sick bird in a hospital cage and lacing its drinking water with potassium iodide (approx. 50gm per liter) over a period of several days. In untreated cases, diseases of the upper respiratory tract can spread into the bronchioles and lungs, causing bronchitis first and finally pneumonia. Cases should not normally be allowed to become so advanced, as the latter condition in particular is extremely difficult to cure and death usually follows. Any serious respiratory problems in birds should be referred to a veterinarian.

One particularly unpleasant disease, fortunately rare in

A red-billed Fawn female.

Zebra Finches, is aspergillosis. It is caused by the fungus *Aspergillus fumigatus,* the spores of which are inhaled and then colonize the lungs and the air sacs. The disease is associated with dusty atmospheres and stale, damp hay. Any hay given to Zebra Finches for nesting purposes should be fresh, clean and sweet smelling. Stored hay should be kept well away from the birds' quarters, and care should be taken when turning or moving hay in the vicinity. Aspergillosis is difficult to diagnose, particularly in its early stages, but will manifest itself in labored breathing as

Passerine pox virus creating raised wart-like lesions on the eyelids of a Goldfinch.

the disease progresses. Treatment with potassium iodide (50gm per liter) in the drinking water may help to prevent or halt the infection if action is taken early enough; but in more severe cases, a veterinarian should be consulted.

Eye Problems
Disorders of the eyes are relatively uncommon in Zebra Finches, but the occasional problem will be heralded by discharges, swelling and obvious discomfort in the bird, which will seek relief by rubbing its eye against a perch or other solid object. Accidental injury to the eye, followed by infection, can cause conjunctivitis, blepharitis or keratitis. The eye may become closed up and inflamed and should be examined carefully for any signs of foreign bodies, which should be removed before washing out with saline solution. Most eye diseases in Zebra Finches respond well to treatment with proprietary eye ointments or drops which should be used according to the manufacturer's instructions.

Lumps

The word *lumps* may sound a little common, but it is usually how abnormal growths on birds are described. As there are so many different kinds of lumps, it is difficult to give them a correct name until one has discovered exactly what

A pair of Florida Fancy Zebra Finches.

before general antibiotic treatment and suture, should the wound be large. Hard lumps may be tumors or growths which can come in two types; one of these is regarded as benign and consists of a single, slow-growing lump, which can often be successfully removed surgically, with no further problem. The other type is known as a malignant, or

they are. Soft lumps on the body are usually a build-up of pus after a scratch or accidental wound which has become infected. Such an abscess may be lanced by a veterinarian, and the wound swabbed out with antiseptic

cancerous, tumor, the cells of which will travel throughout the body, usually resulting in the death of the bird.

Internal tumors, which occasionally occur, are not normally apparent from the outside of the body until it is too late to do anything about them. The causes of such growths are not clearly understood, but in some cases it is suspected that there may be a genetic link. Birds which have or have had tumors should therefore never be used for breeding.

Parasites

Parasites can be described as multicellular organisms which live in or on other organisms from which they obtain food, shelter and other

1. Endoparasites: The only endoparasites which are likely to be of significance to the Zebra Finch keeper are various species of helminthic worms which infest the alimentary canal and include tapeworms, threadworms and roundworms. Most wild, and many aviary, birds have a continual presence of such organisms in their bodies, and under normal healthy conditions they seem to do little harm. Under conditions of stress or disease, however,

Enlargement of a bird louse on a feather. The parasite's glassy eggs are visible at the right.

requirements. There are a number of parasites which may affect Zebra Finches; these may be broadly divided into two categories: endoparasites which live inside the body and ectoparasites which live outside.

worm numbers can increase dramatically and, as the worms feed on partly digested food in the bird's alimentary canal, anemia and weakness can soon set in. The eggs of helminths are passed out in the birds' droppings, and there is the possibility that birds will continually reinfect themselves by feeding from the aviary floor, particularly in the case of earth or turf

Feather lice can be eliminated with commercially prepared powders or sprays available from pet stores.

floors, as opposed to those of concrete, which can be washed down at regular intervals. One method of controlling the eggs of helminths in aviaries is to remove the topsoil annually and to returf.

Infestations of helminths can be easily diagnosed by a veterinary laboratory if regular fecal samples from the birds are supplied. It is possible to worm birds regularly as a preventive measure, but as this is a potentially hazardous operation with small birds, veterinary advice should be sought first.

2. Ectoparasites: These consist of various species of mites, lice or other insects which feed on the blood of the birds by using their biting or piercing mouthparts. In most cases, the parasites reside in nooks and crevices of the cages or aviaries during the day, crawling onto the birds at night in order to feed on their blood. Many such parasites can be carried to aviaries by wild birds which are attracted by seed which may have scattered through the wire. Special insecticidal dusts (which are harmless to the birds) may be obtained from your pet shop and used in cages and aviaries according to the manufacturer's instructions.

One of the most appealing things about keeping Zebra Finches is the number of color varieties which are available and the possibility of becoming involved with, or even producing, a completely new variety. There are about ten well-known varieties and a considerable number of lesser known ones. All color varieties (with the exception of the normal grey) have arisen from mutations which crop up from time to time in wild animals and in captive stock, particularly those that breed prolifically in captivity. The occurrence of mutations in wild animals is one way of providing variations in a population. There are both

Beginners are successful at breeding the prolific Zebra Finch.

advantageous and disadvantageous mutations, the former becoming dominant and the latter usually dying out as a result of natural selection. In wild Zebra Finches, for example, the vast majority of individuals are colored as the "normal grey," although there may be slight geographic variation. The reason for them all being similar in color is that this is the color which is most favorable to the well-being of the population.

To take an extreme example, the occasional white Zebra Finch will crop up in the wild. Such a Zebra Finch will be more susceptible to predatory attack due to its conspicuous color. In addition, it is less likely to be accepted by a member of the opposite sex, due to its unusual appearance, and is therefore less likely to breed and pass on its characteristics to future generations. Even if it does breed, the mutation will be soon overwhelmed by the vast majority of normal birds in the population. In captivity, however, a reverse procedure may take place; the unusual mutation which would not be favored by natural selection in the wild is the delight of the aviculturist, who will make every attempt to proliferate it, improve it, and use it to produce other varieties. Most of the color varieties seen in domestic stock have therefore originated from accidental mutations which have cropped up in the nests of lucky breeders.

Color Breeding
It is not just luck, however, which goes towards producing color varieties suitable for the show bench, and many owners of prize-winning birds may have spent years of hard work, spanning many generations, before the perfect stock emerges. A basic knowledge of genetics is important to those contemplating color breeding. The rules of genetics are similar among all animals (and plants) and were pioneered by

the Austrian biologist Gregor Mendel (1822–1884). Mendel was a priest who studied genetics as a sideline, and it was long after his death that the value of his work was recognized. In 1865, Mendel

Fawn Penguin male; a variety which has a white area stretching from its chin to its vent, creating a penguin appearance.

started his experiments using the common garden pea, a plant which had the advantage of providing a great number of seedlings in each generation, which enabled him to study the relationship between the various types and their hereditary factors. From his studies, Mendel was able to demonstrate the principles governing the transmission of alleles (one of a pair of genes) in two laws: the *law of segregation* and the *law of independent assortment.*

A female Pied Zebra Finch.

There is no room to elucidate more on Mendel's laws here, nor is it necessary to, other than to state that the structures known as genes control all features of an individual, whether it is a pea, a Zebra Finch or even an elephant. The genes are located in the chromosomes,

which are arranged in pairs within the nucleus of the living cells. There are two genes for each characteristic, including color, on opposing chromosomes. In sexual reproduction, female and male reproductive cells (known collectively as gametes), the ova and spermatozoa, fuse together to form zygotes. The gametes each bring half the number of chromosomes found in normal cells, to form a zygote with the correct number of chromosomes for the species. Thus we can see that a young Zebra Finch will inherit characteristics (outward appearance, character, color etc.) from both the mother and the father. The mode of inheritance in Zebra Finches fits into one of three simple groupings.

1. Autosomal Recessive Mutations

The chances of mutations appearing in captive-bred birds increase with the number of offspring. In most cases the normal coloration remains dominant, in which case the mutation is termed "recessive." Should one of a pair of genes mutate for pied, in a strain of normal greys for example, the youngster will have the outward appearance of a normal grey, but will still carry the pied gene in its genetic make-up. Such a bird is termed "grey split for pied" or, more simply, "split pied." It is possible to show

evidence of the mutant gene in future offspring by selective matings.
• Pied x Grey = 100% Grey /Pied.
• Pied x Grey /Pied = 50% Pied + 50% Grey /Pied.
• Pied x Pied = 100% Pied.
• Grey /Pied x Grey = 50% Grey /Pied + 50% Grey.
• Grey /Pied x Grey /Pied = 50% Grey /Pied + 25% Pied + 25% Grey.

2. Sex-Linked Recessive Mutations

These are linked exclusively to the pair of sex chromosomes and, due to the differences in the structure of these between male and female, it is impossible for a hen to be split for a mutation which occurs on part of a male chromosome not paired in the female. Taking fawns and greys as an example, it is not possible to produce a grey /fawn hen, so all grey /fawns in the following examples will be cocks.
• Grey Cock x Fawn Hen = 50% Grey /Fawn Cocks + 50% Grey Hens.
• Grey /Fawn Cock x Grey Hen = 25% Grey Cocks + 25% Grey /Fawn Cocks + 25% Grey Hens + 25% Fawn Hens.
• Grey /Fawn Cock x Fawn Hen = 25% Grey /Fawn Cocks + 25% Fawn Cocks + 25% Grey Hens + 25% Fawn Hens.
• Fawn Cock x Grey Hen = 50% Grey /Fawn Cocks + 50% Fawn Hens.
• Fawn Cock x Fawn Hen = 50% Fawn Cocks + 50% Fawn Hens.

3. Dominant Mutations

In some cases, there are mutations which are dominant to the normal grey, thus reversing the situation of autosomal recessive mutations. Depending on whether one or both genes are mutated, the birds are known as single or double factor (s.f. or d.f.), respectively. Taking dominant creams as an example, the following results can be

The male Pied Zebra Finch.

expected from the pairings indicated.

• Dominant Cream (s.f.) x Grey = 50% Dominant Cream (s.f.) + 50% Grey.

• Dominant Cream (d.f.) x Grey = 100% Dominant Cream (s.f.).

• Dominant Cream (s.f.) x Dominant Cream (s.f.) = 50% Dominant Cream (s.f.) + 25% Dominant Cream (d.f.) + 25% Grey.

• Dominant Cream (s.f.) x Dominant Cream (d.f.) = 50% Dominant Cream (s.f.) + 50% Dominant Cream (d.f.).

• Dominant Cream (d.f.) x Dominant Cream (d.f.) = 100% Dominant Cream (d.f.).

The examples given are based

A female Cream Zebra Finch; the cream coloring may vary from light to dark.

on the average expectancies from large numbers of pairings, so in individual cases results may not be as exact as indicated.

Having taken a brief look at the genetics of color breeding it is now appropriate to discuss the more well-known varieties. Certain color standards are laid down by the various Zebra Finch societies in different countries and these may show slight differences. Those of Great Britain and the United States are similar, however, and possibly the best way to describe the various varieties is to list the standards of a society. The Zebra Finch Society was formed in Great Britain by a small number of dedicated fanciers in 1952 and since then it has grown from strength to strength. It is now one of the largest international specialist societies in the bird fancy. The author is indebted to the secretary of the Zebra Finch Society for giving him permission to reproduce the standards of the Society, as contained in their handbook.

Color Standards (of the Zebra Finch Society)

Normal Cock: Eyes dark. Beak red. Feet and legs red. Head and neck dark grey, wings grey. Breast bar jet black. Throat and upper breast zebra striped, grey with darker lines running from cheek to cheek, continuing down to chest bar. Underparts white; may have

The Cream male Zebra Finch.

some fawnish shading near vent and thighs. Cheek lobes dark orange. Tear markings black and distinct. Tail, black with white bars, side flankings reddish brown with clear white spots.

Normal Hen: As for cock minus chest barring, lobe and flank markings. Beak paler in color. Tear markings, black and distinct. A lighter shade of normal is recognized.

Show faults: Brown shading on wings and mantle.

The Normal or Grey Zebra Finch is the color of Zebra Finches as found in the wild in their native home of Australia. It is from this color that all the other colors of Zebra Finches have been derived, and Normals have been used extensively to improve many colors of Zebras. This unfortunately led to the deterioration of Normals especially with respect to the color of these birds. Due to prompt action taken by several fanciers realizing the dangers, Normals have now almost recovered from this setback. Now many more people keep them for their own particular charm rather than as a means to an end, as was the case some years ago.

It is very difficult to guarantee that Normals are pure and do not mask any other colors; even birds caught in the wild and subsequently bred from in aviaries have produced young of varying colors in their first generations. However, it is important to try and keep Normal stock as pure as possible if the aim is to produce exhibition types.

Fawn Cock: Eyes dark. Beak red. Feet and legs pink. Head, neck and wings deep even fawn. Breast bar dark. Throat

77

Grey Penguin female.

They are probably the longest established mutation of Zebra Finches and are a sex-linked color form.

Pied Cock and Hen: Eyes dark. Beak red. Feet and legs pink. Any other colors to be broken with white approximately 50% of each color (white underparts not to be included in this 50%). Cock to retain cock markings in

Grey Penguin male.

and upper breast light fawn with zebra lines running from cheek to cheek, continuing down to breast bar. Underparts white, may have some fawnish shading near vent and thighs. Cheek lobes dark orange, tear markings same shade as breast bar. Tail dark, barred with white. Side flankings reddish brown with even, clear white spots.

Fawn Hen: As other hens but of the same shade of fawn as cocks.

Show Faults: Variations of color between cock and hen of pairs.

Fawns are the most commonly exhibited color of Zebra Finch and win many specials in open competition.

broken form on cheeks, flanks and chest. Tear marks distinct but can be broken.

Show faults: Loss of cock markings which should be in broken form. Exhibition pairs to be matched for pied markings.

To produce exhibition matched pairs of Pieds is certainly one of the most challenging tasks in the breeding of any exhibition birds. Because the cock and hen of a good show pair must possess the same pied markings, and must still retain 50% of their original color, there are many Pieds bred which never see the show bench.

Pied markings are not passed on to progeny by any known hard-and-fast rules and therefore the appearance of the birds bred is a bit like a lucky dip. Careful planning

The male White Zebra Finch.

can enhance the chance of breeding birds suitable for exhibition purposes but results can never be guaranteed. Pieds can be bred in all colors of Zebra Finches (i.e. Fawn Pieds, Normal Pieds, Cream Pieds,

Penguin Pieds, etc.) but the most favored colors are the Normal Pieds and the Fawn Pieds. This is because they are the only colors where the

The White female has a lighter colored bill.

basic body color is dark enough to contrast effectively with the pied markings. There is not much point in breeding Pieds where the pied markings will appear to be indistinct, as it is the contrast of the bird which makes it so eye catching.

Dominant Silver (Dilute Normal) Cock: Eyes dark. Beak red. Feet and legs pink. There are various shades of dilute normals, silvery grey being the ideal. Chest bars vary from sooty to pale grey, cheek lobes vary from orange to pale cream, flankings from reddish to pinkish fawn with clear, even white spots. Tear markings same shade as breast bar. The lighter the general color the paler the chest, tail, lobes and flankings. Tail dark with white bars.

The Silver male with cheek patch and chest bars apparent.

The female Silver Zebra.

Dominant Silver (Dilute Normal) Hen: As other hens but of the same shade to match the cocks.

Show Faults: Variation in color between cock and hen in pairs and variation in color of individual birds. Fawn shadings. Indistinct markings on cocks.

The term "Dominant" as applied to Dominant Silver does not refer to the color of the birds but the mode of inheritance of this color. There are only two colors of Zebra Finch dominant over the Normal, or wild-type, Zebra Finch which are recognized by the Z.F.S. One is the Dominant Silver and the other is the Dominant Cream.

Dominant Silvers should be exhibited in the Dilute Zebra classes along with Dominant Creams, Recessive Creams and Recessive Silvers; these are, at present, the second most popular color of Dilute Zebra Finch. Dilutes are not as popular now as they were but there are signs that this attractive form of Zebra Finch is about to realize a new wave of popularity.

Dominant Cream (Dilute Fawn) Cock: Eyes dark red. Beak red. Feet and legs pink. Again all shades from deep cream to pale cream.

A pair of Fawn Zebras. The female is preening herself.

of the same shade to match the cocks.

Show Faults: Variation in color between cock and hen of pairs and variation in color of individual birds. Fawn shadings. Indistinct markings on cocks.

The Fawn counterpart of the Dominant Silver is the Dominant Cream. The original Dominant Creams were

Markings in the cock to be in general tone to match depth of diluteness. Tear markings same as breast bar. Tail deep cream with white bars.

Dominant Cream (Dilute Fawn) Hen: As other hens but

produced by pairing fawns to Dominant Silvers. Once seen by fanciers these Creams became very popular. As with Silvers, Creams are not quite as popular now as they have been in the past. Due to the fall in popularity, quality Creams are not found in the numbers they once were and a lot of birds possess undesirable patchiness on the wings.

Recessive Silver (Dilute Normal) Cock: Eyes dark. Beak red. Feet and legs pink. Head, neck and mantle medium bluish grey. Throat and upper breast zebra striped, bluish grey with darker lines running from cheek to cheek continuing down to chest bar. Chest bar dark grey. Tear marks distinct and to match color of chest bar. Cheek lobes medium orange. Underparts white, sometimes slightly shaded near vent and thighs. Flanking light reddish brown with clear white spots. Tail dark with white bars. Cock markings should be clear and distinct with only slight dilution.

Recessive Silver (Dilute Normal) Hen: As other hens but of the same shade to match the cocks.

Show Faults: Variation of color between cock and hen of pairs and variation of color in individual birds. Fawn shadings. Indistinct markings on cock. Color too dark or too light.

This form of dilute is very rarely seen on the show bench and there is probably only a handful of these specimens being used, knowingly, throughout the country. They are however, distinctly different from Dominant Silvers due to the mode of color inheritance. As their name suggests, this form of Dilute is inherited recessively and this is probably one of the reasons for their rarity.

Recessive Cream (Dilute Fawn) Cock: Eyes dark. Beak red. Feet and legs pink. Head, neck and mantle medium cream, wings cream. Throat and upper breast zebra striped, cream with darker lines running from cheek to cheek continuing down to chest bar. Cheek lobes medium orange. Underparts white sometimes slightly shaded near thighs and vent. Flankings light reddish brown with clear white spots. Tail dark cream with white bars.

The male Grey Black-breasted Zebra.

Cock markings should be clear and distinct with only slight dilution.

Recessive Cream (Dilute Fawn) Hens: As other hens but in the same shade to match the cocks.

Show Faults: Variation in color between cock and hen of pairs and variation in color of individual birds. Fawn shadings. Indistinct markings on cocks. Colors too dark or too light.

This is another form of Dilute which is rarely seen on the show bench; however, it is more common than the Recessive Silver form. Recessive Creams are often mistaken for light Fawns, especially those which are bred unsuspectingly from two

A young male Black-breast with markings not fully developed.

A Black-breasted male Zebra.

Fawns. The most misleading feature of this variety is the very prominent cheek patches shown by cock birds which do not resemble those shown by Dominant Creams at all. Add this to the fact that if two Fawns split for Recessive Cream are paired together, which are not known to be split, the beginner expects only Fawns to be produced and has no doubt been informed that light and dark forms of Fawns exist. Recessive Creams do show quite a degree of dilution in their black markings and by comparing the breast marking of the cock with that of a

The Grey Crested female: the crown feathers grow in tufts.

Fawn cock the difference will almost certainly be quite noticeable.

Chestnut Flanked White Cock: Eyes dark. Beak red. Feet and legs pink. Head, neck, back and wings as white as possible. Tear markings same shade as breast bar. Cheek lobes orange. Tail white with bars. Color to match chest bar. Flank markings reddish brown with clear white spots.

Chestnut Flanked White Hen: As other hens to match cocks. May have slight head markings.

Show Faults: Markings too pale in cock.

This color of Zebra Finch was first bred in Australia about 50 years ago and was originally called "Marked White." This name, quite clearly, could have led to confusion among fanciers and the Z.F.S., in their wisdom, decided that the name "Chestnut Flanked White" was more appropriate, and duly named this variety so. In 1968 the Z.F.S. decided that Chestnut Flanked Whites should be exhibited in a class of their own, rather than be exhibited in the A.O.C. class with Whites and Penguins. This measure either led to or coincided with great improvement in the quality of Chestnut Flanked Whites, especially in the coloring of the cock birds, and increased popularity followed to maintain this improvement. The inheritance of the Chestnut Flanked White character is sex-linked and the usual rules which apply to sex-linked varieties apply to Chestnut Flanked Whites.

White Cock and Hen: Eyes dark. Beak red. Feet and legs pink. Pure white all over. Hens usually have beaks of a paler shade of red.

Show Faults: Colored spangles on mantle.

The White Zebra Finch was one of the first mutations of Zebra Finch to appear in captivity but it has not been until recent years that this color has enjoyed popularity on the show bench. For many years, Whites were prone to show dark fleckings in their plumage particularly on their backs. This problem was not satisfactorily overcome until some Whites were bred from Pieds. Technically these birds were White Pieds and the pied markings improved the whiteness of the birds greatly. The whitest birds were of course those that were most heavily pied and when two of these White Pieds were paired together they produced equally white youngsters in the majority of cases.

Another stumbling block with Whites was that many of the whiter birds were rather small and of poor type. Pieds also helped to cure these faults as the good type of the Pieds was transmitted to the White Pieds bred from them. Exhibitors were quick to realize the usefulness of these birds and it was not long before many excellent pairs of Whites were seen on the show bench.

Penguin (Normal) Cock: Eyes dark. Beak red. Feet and legs pink. Head, neck and mantle even silver grey, with flights, secondaries and coverts edged with a paler shade of grey giving a laced effect. (This lacing does not show to full advantage until the second full molt). Underparts from beak to vent pure white without any trace of barring. Cheek lobes pale cream to match body color of the bird. Tail silvery grey barred with white. Side flankings reddish brown with clear white spots.

Penguin (Normal) Hen: As other hens but with cheek lobes white. (There can be Penguin forms in other colors.)

Show Faults: Barring on chest.

This color of Zebra has been quite poorly supported in the past but is now showing signs of increased popularity. Penguins are notorious for being of poor type and being rather on the small side; however, some progress has been made in this direction. The main marking fault in Penguins is chest barrings on the cocks. Since it is an essential feature of this variety to have a pure white front, particular attention must be given to eradicate

A Grey Crested male Zebra Finch.

this fault. Penguins can be bred in all colors, but Normal Penguins and Fawn Penguins are the most popular. Penguins are a recessive variety and this makes them quite hard to establish initially. If Penguins were sex-

A female Fawn Penguin.

linked or even dominant, then it would probably be much easier to improve the standard. As it is, many more of these birds need to be bred before a general overall improvement will be achieved.

More recent additions to the standard list include the Light Backs and the Yellow-Beaked varieties.

Light Backs. Cocks: Eyes dark, beak coral red. Head, neck, back and wings light silvery grey. Throat to upper chest bar black, zebra lines on white ground running from cheek to cheek. Chest bar black. Tear marks black. Cheek lobes medium reddish orange. Underparts below chest bar to vent white with no fawn shading. Tail black with white barrings, side flankings reddish brown ornamented with white spots. Feet and legs deep pink.

Light Backs. Hen: As cock but minus chest markings, flankings and reddish orange ear lobes. Beak paler red. Hens should not have ghost cheek lobes.

Show Faults: Variation in color between cock and hen of pairs and variation in color of individual birds. Fawn shadings. Indistinct markings on cocks.

Yellow-Beaked Varieties: General coloring as Normal Grey and all other mutations, except the beak which should be shades of yellow with the cock birds showing the richest color. There can be a Yellow-beaked form of all the existing mutations and their composite forms. Yellow-beaks must be exhibited in true pairs of the same mutation.

Other varieties which may crop up from time to time include the Crested, which ideally should have a small, neat circular crest similar to that seen in Gloster Fancy Canaries. The Crested may appear in all of the color varieties but the Normal Grey is most common. The Crested character is dominant but unfortunately a lethal factor is involved in the genetic make-up of these birds. Crested birds should therefore always be mated with plain-headed birds and not with each other. The results of normal matings between Crested and plain-headed stock are a mixture of both types. Black-fronted (or Black-brested) Zebra Finches are another variety which may see an increase in popularity. In this type the barring of the chest on cock birds is replaced by a broad, black band. The first Black-breasted

Pied Fawn male.

The female Pied Fawn Zebra.

forms arose in Australia, although an independent strain appeared in Europe more recently.

Exhibition

There comes a time in the life of a breeder of Zebra Finches when he will want to display his birds competitively against other breeders. The first step to take is to join a society which has regular exhibitions. Most societies have exhibitions with beginner and novice classes to enable the newcomer to gain experience in showing. Before actually showing any birds, it will be best to familiarize oneself with the rules and regulations of the society with regard to showing and to study the standards of the various recognized varieties. It will help to visit several shows and to observe the various procedures of benching and judging, and to examine the quality of the birds exhibited. This will give one some ideas of the standards to be aimed at. Do not be worried if your first exhibits do not take prizes; even the most successful of exhibitors had to start somewhere and exhibitions go a long way toward providing the experience required to help one improve one's stock.

Zebra Finches are invariably exhibited in pairs (cock and

A Frosted Grey male.

hen) in standard show cages. Most societies have strict rules regarding the design of the show cages so be sure that you have this correct before entering a show. It requirs quite a bit of preparation to get your birds ready for an exhibition and this should start at least six or seven weeks before the show. Birds of good show type, color and size should be selected, ensuring that any damaged or broken feathers are removed, that nails are not missing or broken and that the birds are in the best of health.

It is best to separate the sexes of birds being prepared for a show, three or four to a cage, and by regular inspection ensure that no fighting occurs. New birds should not be added to a cage with existing birds; all should be placed together into a cage at the same time; the new surroundings will help prevent any squabbling which could be detrimental to the condition of the plumage.

During the period of preparation the birds should be sprayed about once per week with tepid water to which a proprietary plumage conditioner has been added according to the manufacturer's instructions. A further spray should be given about three days before the actual show, so that the plumage is in prime condition. Birds showing feathers in early stages of development (pin feathers) should not be

shown· or they will lose points.
It is better to wait until they
are fully feathered.

It is necessary to "train"
birds which are to be
exhibited. Nervous birds
which flap about the show
cage will not make the judges'
job any easier and they will
probably lose points into the
bargain. Regularly place your
birds into a show cage, so
that they get used to the
interior and used to the
perches. Put your face close
to the wire front and talk to
the birds until they lose their
nervousness as they will have
to get used to a large number
of faces peering at them
during a show. It is also
necessary to get the birds
used to being confined in the
darkness of the transport
boxes, so they should be
placed in their show cages
and put into transport boxes
at regular intervals before the
show. All these little
preparations take up a great

The Crested Penguin female.

deal of time and patience but
it is well worth the effort when
one sees one's first winning
rosette pinned to the cage at
a show.

Top left: *Silver Zebra male;* top right: *Cream Zebra male;* middle: *Grey Normal Zebra male;* bottom left: *White Zebra male;* bottom right: *Fawn Zebra male.*

ALL ABOUT FINCHES AND RELATED SEED-EATING BIRDS by Ian Harman and Dr. Matthew M. Vriends (PS-765)

More than 100 finches and other seed-eating birds are fully identified with a helpful commentary on how they adapt to captivity and their breeding requirements. Chapters on housing and management, feeding, and keeping birds healthy are followed by treatments of the following groups: true finches, buntings, cardinals and grosbeaks, weavers and whydahs, waxbills, and grass-finches, parrot finches, and mannikins.
Illustrated with 53 color and 65 black-and-white photos. Hard cover, 5½" × 8", 224 pp.

FINCHES AND SOFT-BILLED BIRDS by Henry Bates and Robert Busenbark (H-908)

The classic reference on finches and soft-bills. Every important cage bird (except parrots) is discussed and illustrated in color. No other book in any language has so many birds known in the pet world. Used extensively all over the world as an identification guide, this book also covers all the fundamentals of maintaining and breeding these species.
Illustrated with 246 color and 159 black-and-white photograhs. Hard cover, 5½" × 8", 735 pp.

BREEDING ZEBRA FINCHES by Mervin F. Roberts (KW-056)

General information is provided on the care and management of Zebra Finches for the successful breeding of these birds. The courtship, and nesting habits, fostering of young; and the general nourishment and housing of finches are covered. An extensive section on genetics details the color varieties that can be created through crossbreeding. Also included is a discussion on interbreeding Zebra Finches with other finch species. Written for simplicity in an easy to understand format, directed at both the novice and the experienced breeder. Bound in a small, easily handled and referenced edition.
Illustrated with 49 color and 32 black-and-white photos. Hard cover, 5½" × 8", 96 pp.

ZEBRA FINCHES by Melvin F. Roberts (KW-055)

Melvin F. Roberts expands on the care and nutritional requirements of the Zebra Finch. Food supplements, minerals, grit and vitamins for the healthy upkeep of these finches are covered.
For those ready to exhibit their newly produced offspring in color competition, there is a copy of the "Standards of the Zebra Finch Society—Show Standards. Detailed are the required color markings needed for competition; two pages of line drawings are devoted to illustrating the Society's standard show cage. Also included is an interesting chapter on the life cycle of these prolific and popular finches. Must reading for those who wish to expand their knowledge of Zebra Finches, as well as those interested in exhibiting these birds.
Illustrated with 76 color and 38 black-and-white photos, line drawings included. Hard cover, 5½" × 8", 96 pp.

Index

A COMPLETE INTRODUCTION TO
ZEBRA FINCHES

Variations in male Zebra Finches created through crossbreeding.